McGraw-Hill Reading/Langu...
TEACHER'S MANUA...

Comprehensive Assessment Blackline Masters and Teacher's Manual

CONTENTS

Overview

McGraw-Hill Reading provides a complete array of performance-based assessment instruments to support instruction. A wide variety of assessment information may be collected, organized, and evaluated through the use of the **Assessment Portfolio**.

In McGraw-Hill Reading, *performance assessment* implies the use of multiple measures in a wide variety of authentic situations to evaluate what students can do. Information collected through various forms of assessment, including tests, is used for *evaluation*, or making judgments about student performance. *Portfolios* provide a tool and a method for organizing and evaluating the results of various assessments.

Performance assessment and the use of portfolios offer wonderful opportunities to achieve greater insights for both students and teachers. A comprehensive profile of each student includes both formal and informal assessments, such as teacher observations, performance tasks, writing samples, classroom activities, reading assessments, and self-assessments.

Our approach to assessment is based on the following principles:

◆ Assessment should be closely integrated with instruction.

◆ Assessment should be based on the notion of *progress*—evaluating student progress toward achieving the goals and outcomes of instruction.

◆ Assessment should be continuous, throughout the school year, and should incorporate a wide variety of modes and types of assessment.

◆ Assessment tasks and activities should be direct and authentic, reflecting what students actually need to be able to do.

◆ Authentic assessment activities should involve all of the integrated language arts: reading, writing, listening, speaking, and viewing.

◆ The program should emphasize self-assessment and cooperative efforts between teacher and students, among student peers, and involving parents.

Introduction

The Concept of Progress

McGraw-Hill Reading emphasizes strategy-based instruction in reading and integrated language arts, including writing, listening, speaking, and viewing. Strategy-based instruction teaches students to use thinking processes; it differs significantly from skill-based instruction, which teaches isolated skills.

The strategy-based approach has profound implications for assessment. The foundation of the program, reading as a process of constructing meaning, does not change significantly from one grade to another; what changes is the complexity of the reading material and the sophistication with which students apply strategies. Essentially, the assessment component is designed to measure this concept of gradual progress, to ensure that students meet the program goals and outcomes at each level.

Each Unit Assessment provides an integrated set of activities emphasizing literature and authentic performance tasks, and these activities are based on reading, writing, and listening strategies. Each assessment includes:

◆ Literature selections and comprehension questions

◆ Vocabulary strategies

◆ Study skills

◆ Listening comprehension tasks

◆ Writing activity

Assessment Options

Portfolio-based assessment incorporates a variety of both formal and informal measures. Formal assessments of reading, writing, and listening include:

◆ Unit Assessment

◆ Mid-Year Assessment

◆ End-Year Assessment

There are several ways to use these assessments. Two recommended alternatives are described below. Either approach will help provide a profile of a student's progress throughout the school year. For the assessment in each unit, there are two forms:

The **Multiple-Choice** form, which consists of traditional multiple-choice questions and writing prompt.

The **Comprehension Prompt**, which requires an extended written response to a literature selection. The Comprehension Prompts spark a separate response to each of the selections in the Unit Assessment.

Assess after each unit or at Mid-Year and End-Year. Your choice from among the forms might be determined as follows:

◆ If you want or need a quick-scoring test, the Multiple-Choice form might be most effective.

◆ If you want to assess students' abilities to write extended responses to literature— without the study skills and listening tasks—then the Comprehension Prompts would probably work best for you.

◆ All forms of the Unit Assessments are designed as formal assessments. However, you may choose to use them in other ways. For example, the Comprehension Prompts may be used as group discussion topics or as topics for independent writing.

Scheduling Assessment

You may choose to give an entire assessment in two or more sittings, or you may choose to give only some parts.

Deciding which parts to administer will depend mainly on whether students have received instruction and/or need practice on the content measured by each part.

The Unit Assessments are not intended to be timed. However, for scheduling and planning purposes, the chart below shows the number of questions and the estimated time required to administer the complete assessment. (For more detailed information about each assessment, see later sections of this manual.)

Assessment	Domain	No. Items	Testing Schedule	Time (Mins.)
Unit Assessments *(to be used after each unit to help determine the progress each student has made during the unit of instruction)*	Comprehension Vocabulary Strategy Study Skills Listening Writing	1–4, 7–10, 13–16 5–6, 11–12, 17–18 19–22 23–25		60 8 15 15
Mid-Year & End-Year Assessments *(to measure cumulative progress midway and at the end of the year)*	Comprehension Vocabulary Strategy *Study Skills* Listening Writing	1–6, 11–16, 21–26, 31–36 7–10, 17–20, 27–30 37–45 46–50	**Day 1:** Comprehension and Vocabulary Strategy **Day 2:** Study Skills, Listening, and Writing	80 45

Teacher's Notes

_____

_____

_____

_____

_____

_____

_____

_____

_____

_____

_____

_____

_____

_____

_____

_____

_____

_____

_____

_____

_____

_____

_____

_____

_____

_____

Administering the Assessments

Administration Procedures

In a criterion-referenced assessment, it is critical for students to understand exactly what they are expected to do. You should become familiar with the directions in this manual and with the test questions before giving the assessment in order to administer these tests efficiently and make the directions understandable to students.

Before testing, make sure that each student has a copy of the assessment booklet. For most of the assessment, students may either write their answers directly in the booklets or on separate pieces of paper.

During the test, monitor students' test-taking behavior to make sure that each student is following the directions, is on the correct question, and is writing responses in the correct places. You should feel comfortable answering questions about procedures and materials, but not helping them answer the questions or understand what they are reading.

After testing, make sure that each student has written his or her name on the test booklet and/or on the separate piece of paper used to write responses.

Specific directions for administering the assessments begin on the next page.

In the directions that follow, the sections in *italic* print are intended to be read aloud to students. The rest of the directions are intended for the teacher only and should not be read aloud.

Unit 1
The Middle of Nowhere, p. 3

Have students open their Unit Assessments to page 3. Say: *You will read a story called "The Middle of Nowhere" and then answer some questions. Read all four answer choices for each question. Then fill in the circle next to the right answer. When you have finished, put down your pencils and look at me. You may begin now.*

Have students read the story and answer questions 1–6 on page 4.

The Birthday Present, p. 5

When all the students have finished answering the questions on page 4, have them turn to page 5. Say: *Now you will read a story called "The Birthday Present" and then answer some questions. Read all four answer choices for each question. Then fill in the circle next to the right answer. When you have finished, put down your pencils and look at me. You may begin now.*

Have students read the story and answer questions 7–12 on page 6.

Treasure Hunters, p. 7

When all students have completed the questions on page 6, have them turn to page 7. Say: *Now you will read a story called "Treasure Hunters" and then answer some questions. Read all four answer choices for each question. Then fill in the circle next to the right answer. When you have finished, put down your pencils and look at me. You may begin now.*

Have students read the story and answer questions 13–18 on page 8.

Study Skills, pp. 9–10

Have students turn to page 9. Check to see that all students are on the correct page. Say: *Look over the glossary pictured on page 9. Then, use the information in the glossary to answer questions 19 and 20 at the bottom of this page. Read all four answer choices for each question. Then fill in the circle next to the right answer. When you have finished, put down your pencils and look at me. You may begin now.*

When all the students have finished answering the questions on page 9, have them turn to page 10.

Now look over the sample index pictured on page 10. Then, use the information in the index to answer questions 21 and 22 at the bottom of this page. Read all of the answer choices for each question. Then fill in the circle next to the right answer. When you have finished, put down your pencils and look at me. You may begin now.

Listening, p. 11

When students are ready, have them turn to page 11 and read the directions at the top of the page. Say: *You are going to hear a story. I will read part of it and ask a question. Fill in the circle next to the correct answer. Listen carefully. We will begin now.*

The Fool-Proof Cake

Carmen paced up and back as she waited for Scott. "He'd better hurry," she muttered. "The bake sale is just a few hours away."

Sometimes Scott drove her crazy, the way he always put things off. "It's about time," she snapped when Scott finally ambled in.

"Take it easy," he answered calmly. "We've got plenty of time. Now where's this fool-proof fudge cake recipe you've been talking about?"

"Right here," Carmen said. "And I got out all the stuff we'll need. This cake is delicious, and it'll help the soccer team make money for new equipment."

Now I will stop and ask you a question. Find question 23 at the top of the page.

Here is question 23. In the story, Scott ambled in. What does ambled *mean? Choose your answer.*

Now listen as I read the rest of the story to you. Listen carefully.

As she and Scott worked, Carmen's mood improved.

"The cake has to bake for half an hour," she explained. "We'll frost it after it cools. We'll have just enough time." Just then, the light above the counter blew out.

"Scott, the light is too high for me to reach. Will you change the bulb?" Carmen asked.

"Later," he replied. "I'm going to make the frosting now."

Carmen sighed and said, "I think I'll go wash up while I wait for the cake to bake— and for you to finish the frosting."

When Carmen walked back into the kitchen, Scott told her that the frosting was done. He had a funny look on his face. Carmen looked into the bowl that Scott was holding.

"What happened?" she gasped. "That doesn't look like frosting! It looks like chocolate soup!"

"I think I read the recipe wrong," said Scott. "Do you think the light was too dim? Maybe I'll change that bulb now."

Carmen didn't answer as she threw out the ruined frosting. Then she said softly, "Scott, only you could ruin a fool-proof cake!"

Find question 24. Here is the question: What do you think Carmen will do next? Choose your answer.

Now look at question 25. Here is the question: This story is mostly about two people who _____. Choose your answer.

Writing Prompt, p. 12

When students are ready, have them turn to page 12. Check to see that all students are on the correct page. Say: *Now you are going to write a paragraph on this page. Read the directions silently while I read them aloud. Write a story about the first birthday you can remember. Describe what your day was like and how it felt to be one year older.*

Make sure students understand what they are expected to do.

When you have finished writing, put down your pencils and look at me. You may begin writing now.

Unit 2
The Secret Cave, p. 3

Have students open their Unit Assessments to page 3. Say: *You will read a story called "The Secret Cave" and then answer some questions. Read all four answer choices for each question. Then fill in the circle next to the right answer. When you have finished, put down your pencils and look at me. You may begin now.*

Have students read the story and answer questions 1–6 on page 4.

Hands Across Time, p. 5

When all the students have finished answering the questions on page 4, have them turn to page 5. Say: *Now you will read a story called "Hands Across Time" and then answer some questions. Read all four answer choices for each question. Then fill in the circle next to the right answer. When you have finished, put down your pencils and look at me. You may begin now.*

Have students read the story and answer questions 7–12 on page 6.

The Golden Cloak, p. 7

When all students have completed the questions on page 6, have them turn to page 7. Say: *Now you will read a story called "The Golden Cloak" and then answer some questions. Read all four answer choices for each question. Then fill in the circle next to the right answer. When you have finished, put down your pencils and look at me. You may begin now.*

Have students read the story and answer questions 13–18 on page 8.

Study Skills, pp. 9–10

Have students turn to page 9. Check to see that all students are on the correct page. Say: *On page 9, you will see a sample entry from a dictionary. Look this over, then use the information in the dictionary entry to answer questions 19 and 20 at the bottom of this page. Read all of the answer choices for each question. Then fill in the circle next to the right answer. When you have finished, put down your pencils and look at me. You may begin now.*

When all the students have finished answering the questions on page 9, have them turn to page 10.

On page 10, you will see a sample index from an encyclopedia. Look over the index, then use the information in it to answer questions 21 and 22 at the bottom of page 10. Read all four answer choices for each question. Then fill in the circle next to the right answer. When you have finished, put down your pencils and look at me. You may begin now.

Listening, p. 11

When students are ready, have them turn to page 11 and read the directions at the top of the page. Say: *You are going to hear a story. I will read part of it and ask a question. Fill in the circle next to the correct answer. Listen carefully. We will begin now.*

Wolf Plays a Trick

Long ago, when all the animals spoke the same language, Wolf spent his time trying to trick the others into becoming his next meal.

One day, Wolf had a new scheme. He couldn't wait to try it out. He didn't have to wait long. As Mouse went past his cave, Wolf poked his head out and said, "Mouse!" You're just the fellow I wanted to see. I need your great strength to help me put my new thingamabob together."

Delighted, Mouse flexed his puny arms and said, "Oh, of course, Wolf, of course." And he scampered into Wolf's cave.

Now I will stop and ask you a question. Find question 23 at the top of the page.

Here is question 23: Mouse flexed his puny arms. What does puny mean? Choose your answer.

Now listen as I read the rest of the story to you. Listen carefully.

Next came Goose. This time Wolf said, "I'm so happy to see you, dear Goose. I need your great mind to help me put my new thingamabob together."

Honking with pleasure, silly Goose said, "Why I'm sure I can figure it out." And she waddled into Wolf's cave.

Pretty soon Donkey ambled along. "Dear Donkey," Wolf said. "What a fine coincidence. I need your delicate touch to help me put my new thingamabob together."

Donkey pawed the ground happily with his huge hooves. "How can I refuse a friend in need?" he said. And he galloped into the cave.

The next day, Rabbit was passing by. Wolf was ready for her. "Rabbit, my friend," said Wolf. "I need your amazing strength to help me put my new thingamabob together."

"Forgive me for not staying," replied timid Rabbit, "but false praise always frightens me." And she hopped away as fast as she could.

MORAL: Never trust a flatterer.

Find question 24. Here is the question: You can predict that Wolf will _____. Choose your answer.

Now look at question 25. Here is the question: "Never trust a flatterer" mostly means that _____. Choose your answer.

Writing Prompt, p. 12

When students are ready, have them turn to page 12. Check to see that all students are on the correct page. Say: *Now you are going to write a paragraph on this page. Read the directions silently while I read them aloud. You want to start an after-school club in an area that interests you. Write a letter to your principal about the club you'd like to start. Explain why you think it would be a good club and persuade your principal to let you start it.*

Make sure students understand what they are expected to do.

When you have finished writing, put down your pencils and look at me. You may begin writing now.

Unit 3
Stan Herd, Crop Artist, p. 3

Have students open their Unit Assessments to page 3. Say: *You will read a story called "Stan Herd, Crop Artist" and then answer some questions. Read all four answer choices for each question. Then fill in the circle next to the right answer. When you have finished, put down your pencils and look at me. You may begin now.*

Have students read the story and answer questions 1–6 on page 4.

Tracy's New Computer, p. 5

When all the students have finished answering the questions on page 4, have them turn to page 5. Say: *Now you will read a story called "Tracy's New Computer" and then answer some questions. Read all four answer choices for each question. Then fill in the circle next to the right answer. When you have finished, put down your pencils and look at me. You may begin now.*

Have students read the story and answer questions 7–12 on page 6.

Johnny Appleseed, p. 7

When all students have completed the questions on page 6, have them turn to page 7. Say: *Now you will read a story called "Johnny Appleseed" and then answer some questions. Read all four answer choices for each question. Then fill in the circle next to the right answer. When you have finished, put down your pencils and look at me. You may begin now.*

Have students read the story and answer questions 13–18 on page 8.

Study Skills, pp. 9–10

Have students turn to page 9. Check to see that all students are on the correct page. Say: *Look over the family tree pictured on page 9. Then, use the information in the family tree to answer questions 19 and 20 at the bottom of this page. Read all four answer choices for each question. Then fill in the circle next to the right answer. When you have finished, put down your pencils and look at me. You may begin now.*

When all the students have finished answering the questions on page 9, have them turn to page 10.

On page 10, you will see a drawing that shows growth rings on trees. Look over the drawing, then use the information in it to answer questions 21 and 22 at the bottom of the page. Read all four answer choices for each question. Then fill in the circle next to the right answer. When you have finished, put down your pencils and look at me. You may begin now.

Listening, p. 11

When students are ready, have them turn to page 11 and read the directions at the top of the page. Say: *You are going to hear a story. I will read part of it and ask a question. Fill in the circle next to the correct answer. Listen carefully. We will begin now.*

April Fools

Jackie was cautious as he got out of bed. It was April Fool's Day. His mother was an avid trickster. Each year she found ways to trick him throughout the day. Now he thought he knew most of her tricks. But there were always new ones.

When Jackie stood up out of bed he jumped two feet off the ground when he heard popping sounds. He was standing on bubble wrap that his mother had placed on the floor all around his bed. That was a new one. When he put on his shirt, his hands hit a dead-end. The sleeves were sewn shut. Sighing, he opened his door and walked into the newspaper taped over the doorway.

In the kitchen, Jackie tried puffed rice cereal rather than risk finding something awful in the corn flakes he usually ate. It was no use. There were rubber bugs in the puffed rice. And when he poured the milk, it was blue. Could he trust the donuts on the counter? One bite told him he couldn't. They were made of play dough.

Now I will stop and ask you a question. Find question 23 at the top of the page.

Here is question 23: His mother was an avid trickster. The word avid *means _____. Choose your answer.*

Now listen as I read the rest of the story to you. Listen carefully.

A giggle made Jackie look up. It was his mother. "It's time to go," she said. "Get your lunch and I'll drive you to school."

"Like I'm really going to eat what's in that bag," Jackie replied. "Last year you put toothpaste in my sandwich cookies." His mother just looked innocent.

"Someday I'll get you back," he said.

"I bet you won't," she said with a smile. "I'm much too clever for you.

Jackie and his mother walked out to the car. As she was getting in, she noticed six quarters and a shiny half dollar lying on the sidewalk. She reached down to pick them up. But she couldn't lift them. Someone had glued them to the ground.

Now it was Jackie's turn to look innocent.

Find question 24. Here is the question: How do you think Jackie's mother reacted to his trick? Choose your answer.

Now look at question 25. Here is the question: What is this story mainly about? Choose your answer.

Writing Prompt, p. 12

When students are ready, have them turn to page 12. Check to see that all students are on the correct page. Say: *Now you are going to write a paragraph on this page. Read the directions silently while I read them aloud. Write a report on how to put on a class play.*

Make sure students understand what they are expected to do.

When you have finished writing, put down your pencils and look at me. You may begin writing now.

Unit 4
Sharks, p. 3

Have students open their Unit Assessments to page 3. Say: *You will read a story called "Sharks" and then answer some questions. Read all four answer choices for each question. Then fill in the circle next to the right answer. When you have finished, put down your pencils and look at me. You may begin now.*

Have students read the story and answer questions 1–6 on page 4.

Birthday Sky, p. 5

When all the students have finished answering the questions on page 4, have them turn to page 5. Say: *Now you will read a story called "Birthday Sky" and then answer some questions. Read all four answer choices for each question. Then fill in the circle next to the right answer. When you have finished, put down your pencils and look at me. You may begin now.*

Have students read the story and answer questions 7–12 on page 6.

Mrs. Miller's Machine, p. 7

When all the students have finished answering the questions on page 6, have them turn to page 7. Say: *Now you will read a story called "Mrs. Miller's Machine" and then answer some questions. Read all four answer choices for each question. Then fill in the circle next to the right answer. When you have finished, put down your pencils and look at me. You may begin now.*

Have students read the story and answer questions 13–18 on page 8.

Study Skills, pp. 9–10

Have students turn to page 9. Check to see that all students are on the correct page. Say: *Look over the map on this page. Then use the information in the map to answer questions 19 and 20 at the bottom of this page. When you have finished, put down your pencils and look at me. You may begin now.*

When all the students have finished answering the questions on page 9, have them turn to page 10.

Look over the diagram titled "Lifting Loads Safely." Then use the information in the diagram to answer questions 21 and 22 at the bottom of the page. When you have finished, put down your pencils and look at me. You may begin now.

Listening, p. 11

When students are ready, have them turn to page 11 and read the directions at the top of the page. Say: *You are going to hear a story. I will read part of it and ask a question. Fill in the circle next to the correct answer. Listen carefully. We will begin now.*

Investigating Insects

During the summer, there are always a lot of insects flying around. One day I decided to see how many different insects I could find in my own yard. I grabbed a magnifying glass and a book about insects. Then I headed outside.

The first thing I saw was a butterfly. Butterflies are the most beautiful insects. They are active by day and feed on flower nectar. Adult butterflies live for about one month.

As I walked through the garden, I saw a grasshopper chewing on a tomato plant. Grasshoppers have powerful back legs that they use for hopping. Some grasshoppers grow to 4 inches in length.

A buzzing sound drew my eyes toward a squash flower. Inside the flower was a fat, yellow bee. It was eating the pollen it found there. When bees and other insects fly from flower to flower, they spread bits of pollen around. This process, called cross-pollination, is necessary for plants to turn flowers into fruits and vegetables.

Now I will stop and ask you a question. Find question 23 at the top of the page.

Here is question 23: From this passage you can say the writer _____. Choose your answer.

Now listen as I read the rest of the story to you. Listen carefully.

I thought I had seen just about all the insects, when a tiny patch of red caught my eye. It was a ladybird beetle resting on a rose leaf. These beetles, which have red bodies with black spots, are friends to all gardeners. You see, they feed on plant-eating insects.

Luckily, I didn't see any mosquitoes while I was outside. They are simply the worst pests. Most times, I don't need my magnifying glass to know that mosquitoes are around. I can tell by the red, itchy bumps on my arms and legs.

Find question 24. Here is the question: What conclusion can you draw about insects from this passage? Choose your answer.

Now look at question 25. Here is the question: The narrator used a magnifying glass. A magnifying glass is a tool for _____. Choose your answer.

Writing Prompt, p. 12

When students are ready, have them turn to page 12. Check to see that students are on the correct page. Say: *Now you are going to write a paragraph on this page. Read the directions silently while I read them aloud. Write a report on surprising facts about sharks to present to your class. Use the story "Sharks" to help you write your report.*

Make sure students understand what they are expected to do.

When you have finished writing, put down your pencils and look at me. You may begin writing now.

Unit 5
A Room for Two, p. 3

Have students open their Unit Assessments to page 3. Say: *You will read a story called "A Room for Two" and then answer some questions. Read all four answer choices for each question. Then fill in the circle next to the right answer. When you have finished, put down your pencils and look at me. You may begin now.*

Have students read the story and answer questions 1–6 on page 4.

The First Shoes, p. 5

When all the students have finished answering the questions on page 4, have them turn to page 5. Say: *Now you will read a story called "The First Shoes" and then answer some questions. Read all four answer choices for each question. Then fill in the circle next to the right answer. When you have finished, put down your pencils and look at me. You may begin now.*

Have students read the story and answer questions 7–12 on page 6.

What to Buy Rover?, p. 7

When all the students have finished answering the questions on page 6, have them turn to page 7. Say: *Now you will read a story called "What to Buy Rover?" and then answer some questions. Read all four answer choices for each question. Then fill in the circle next to the right answer. When you have finished, put down your pencils and look at me. You may begin now.*

Have students read the story and answer questions 13–18 on page 8.

Study Skills, pp. 9–10

Have students turn to page 9. Check to see that all students are on the correct page. Say: *Look over the newspaper article on page 9. Take a moment to study the headline, then read the article. Use the information in the article to answer questions 19 and 20 at the bottom of this page. When you have finished, put down your pencils and look at me. You may begin now.*

When all the students have finished answering the questions on page 9, have them turn to page 10.

Read the newspaper editorial on page 10. Use the information in the editorial to answer questions 21 and 22 at the bottom of the page. When you have finished, put down your pencils and look at me. You may begin now.

Listening, p. 11

When students are ready, have them turn to page 11 and read the directions at the top of the page. Say: *You are going to hear a story. I will read part of it and ask a question. Fill in the circle next to the correct answer. Listen carefully. We will begin now.*

A Great Idea

The first time I saw the beach, I felt frightened of the waves. I waded into the water only until it was up to my knees. My little sister bravely swam past me into the deep water, my mother at her side. They splashed and dived into the waves. They kept calling to me, "Amanda, come in. It's fun!"

I decided to build a sand castle. That was fun, too, but I felt a little ashamed.

A week later, we went back to the beach. I made up my mind in the car that this time I would go into the deep water. I waded in bravely with my sister and mother. But when the water was up to my waist, I stepped on something rough. My imagination went wild. I swam back to the shallow water and played there the rest of the day. I was upset with myself when we left that day.

Now I will stop and ask you a question. Find question 23 at the top of the page.

Here is question 23: The water was shallow. This means that it was —————. *Choose your answer.*

Now listen as I read the rest of the story to you. Listen carefully.

Luckily, my aunt invited my family to go back to the beach two weeks later. I was determined to swim in the deep water. I even came up with an idea to ease my fears. I packed my oldest pair of sneakers in the bag with our towels. I didn't tell anybody about this.

When it was time to swim, I slipped the shoes on my feet. For some reason, the shoes made me feel safe in the deep water. I splashed and swam for about an hour. When I walked out of the water, everyone looked surprised to see that I was wearing shoes. But no one has ever said anything about it.

Find question 24. Here is the question: What do you think Amanda will do from now on? Choose your answer.

Now look at question 25. Here is the question: This story is mainly about —————. *Choose your answer.*

Writing Prompt, p. 12

When students are ready, have them turn to page 12. Check to see that students are on the correct page. Say: *Now you are going to write a paragraph on this page. Read the directions silently while I read them aloud. Write a report comparing a subject you enjoy studying in school with one you don't like that much. Compare and contrast the two subjects and explain what makes one more interesting than the other.*

Make sure students understand what they are expected to do.

When you have finished writing, put down your pencils and look at me. You may begin writing now.

Unit 6
Jazz Giant, p. 3

Have students open their Unit Assessments to page 3. Say: *You will read a story called "Jazz Giant" and then answer some questions. Read all four answer choices for each question. Then fill in the circle next to the right answer. When you have finished, put down your pencils and look at me. You may begin now.*

Have students read the story and answer questions 1–6 on page 4.

Breaking into Broadcasting, p. 5

When all the students have finished answering the questions on page 4, have them turn to page 5. Say: *Now you will read a story called "Breaking into Broadcasting" and then answer some questions. Read all four answer choices for each question. Then fill in the circle next to the right answer. When you have finished, put down your pencils and look at me. You may begin now.*

Have students read the story and answer questions 7–12 on page 6.

Devin's Decision, p. 7

When all the students have finished answering the questions on page 6, have them turn to page 7. Say: *Now you will read a story called "Devin's Decision" and then answer some questions. Read all four answer choices for each question. Then fill in the circle next to the right answer. When you have finished, put down your pencils and look at me. You may begin now.*

Have students read the story and answer questions 13–18 on page 8.

Study Skills, pp. 9–10

Have students turn to page 9. Check to see that all students are on the correct page. Say: *Read the outline on this page. Use the information in the outline to answer questions 19 and 20 at the bottom of this page. When you have finished, put down your pencils and look at me. You may begin now.*

When all the students have finished answering the questions on page 9, have them turn to page 10.

On page 10, you will see several resources that can be found in the library, as well as a sample entry from one of these resources. Use what you know about these resources to answer questions 21 and 22 at the bottom of the page. When you have finished, put down your pencils and look at me. You may begin now.

Listening, p. 11

When students are ready, have them turn to page 11 and read the directions at the top of the page. Say: *You are going to hear a story. I will read part of it and ask a question. Fill in the circle next to the correct answer. Listen carefully. We will begin now.*

On the Trail

My dream quickly became a nightmare. Had I made the worst decision of my life? My uncle's tales of adventure on cattle drives had sparked dreams in me. I couldn't wait until I was old enough to be a cowboy. Finally, when I was seventeen, I got hired to help drive a thousand longhorns from Texas to Kansas.

There I was, in the middle of a raging storm. Lightning split the sky. A rumbling noise filled the air around us. Then I heard the cry: "STAMPEDE!!" Everything went crazy around me.

Hours later I found myself lost and alone with my horse and 70 cows. Soon the trail boss showed up. He didn't say a word as we drove the cattle back to the main herd. "Get something to eat," he finally said.

We still had a long way to go. I was beginning to see that the cowboy life was far from glamorous. Every day, I rode with other young cowboys, behind the slowest cattle, breathing dust all the way.

Now I will stop and ask you a question. Find question 23 at the top of the page.

Here is question 23: Cowboy life was far from glamorous. The word glamorous *means ———. Choose your answer.*

Now listen carefully as I read the rest of the story to you.

The day after the stampede, we drove the cattle across the Red River. The water churned as we forced the longhorns to swim across the river. I felt that any second I might be thrown from my horse into the middle of the terrified animals.

Finally, we arrived in Abilene, Kansas. I helped load the cattle on a train. Then I collected my pay and rode back home. I thought about the cowboy life all the way home. I'm not sure if it's the life for me.

Find question 24. Here is the question: This passage is mainly about ———. Choose your answer.

Now look at question 25. Here is the question: You might guess that the youngest cowboys ———. Choose your answer.

Writing Prompt, p. 12

When students are ready, have them turn to page 12. Check to see that students are on the correct page. Say: *Now you are going to write a paragraph on this page. Read the directions silently while I read them aloud. Imagine that your family's car could talk. What do you think it would say? Write a story about a day in the life of your car, from your car's point of view.*

Make sure students understand what they are expected to do.

When you have finished writing, put down your pencils and look at me. You may begin writing now.

Mid-Year
A Fun Way to Remember, p. 3

Have students open their Unit Assessments to page 3. Say: *You will read a story called "A Fun Way to Remember" and then answer some questions. Read all four answer choices for each question. Then fill in the circle next to the right answer. When you have finished, put down your pencils and look at me. You may begin now.*

Have students read the story and answer questions 1–10 on pages 4 and 5.

Fitting In, p. 6

When all the students have finished answering the questions on pages 4 and 5, have them turn to page 6. Say: *Now you will read a story called "Fitting In" and then answer some questions. Read all four answer choices for each question. Then fill in the circle next to the right answer. When you have finished, put down your pencils and look at me. You may begin now.*

Have students read the story and answer questions 11–20 on pages 7 and 8.

The Storage Closet, p. 9

When all students have completed the questions on pages 7 and 8, have them turn to page 9. Say: *Now you will read a story called "The Storage Closet" and then answer some questions. Read all four* answer choices for each question. Then fill in the circle next to the right answer. When you have finished, put down your pencils and look at me. You may begin now.

Have students read the story and answer questions 21–30 on pages 10 and 11.

Jacqueline's Gift, p. 12

When all students have completed the questions on pages 10 and 11, have them turn to page 12. Say: *Now you will read a story called "Jacqueline's Gift" and then answer some questions. Read all four answer choices for each question. Then fill in the circle next to the right answer. When you have finished, put down your pencils and look at me. You may begin now.*

Have students read the story and answer questions 31–36 on page 13.

Study Skills, pp. 14–19

Have students turn to page 14. Check to see that all students are on the correct page. Say: *On page 14, you will see parts of a glossary and an index. Look these over carefully. Then, use the information in the glossary and the index to answer questions 37–39 on page 15. Read all four answer choices for each question. Then fill in the circle next to the right answer. When you have finished, put down your pencils and look at me. You may begin now.*

When all the students have finished answering the questions on page 15, have them turn to page 16.

Read the caption and look over the map on page 16. Then, use the information in the map to answer questions 40–42 on page 17. Read all of the answer choices for each question. Then fill in the circle next to the right answer. When you have finished, put down your pencils and look at me. You may begin now.

When all the students have finished answering the questions on page 17, have them turn to page 18.

On page 18 you will see a drawing of a small table. Look over the drawing, then use the information in it to answer questions 43–45 on page 19. Read all of the answer choices for each question. Then fill in the circle next to the right answer. When you have finished, put down your pencils and look at me. You may begin now.

Listening, p. 20

When students are ready, have them turn to page 20 and read the directions at the top of the page. Say: *You are going to hear a story. I will read part of it and ask two questions. Fill in the circle next to the correct answer. Listen carefully. We will begin now.*

Jan had never had a science teacher like Mrs. Gates before. She sometimes carried a grass snake wrapped around her arm, and she spent every free minute at her desk, hammering on rocks. Ching, ching, it rang in the halls when Jan's class went out for recess. Strangest of all, Mrs. Gates never, ever smiled. When Jan commented on this to her friend, Brian, he said, "She's a little different, but I like her."

"She scares me a little," said Jan.

Then Jan forgot her science homework. When Mrs. Gates told her to come in and do it during recess, she told Brian, "I hope she doesn't have that snake."

"Don't worry," joked Brian, "I think there's a rule against teachers feeding kids to their pet snakes."

Jan opened the door to Mrs. Gates's room, and relaxed when she saw the snake in its terrarium. Mrs. Gates had her nose buried in her rocks, but mumbled, "Go on and get started, Jan. Let me know if you need assistance."

Now I will stop and ask you two questions. Find question 46 at the top of the page.

Here is question 46: Jan relaxed when she saw the snake in its terrarium. The word terrarium *means ——————. Choose your answer.*

Find question 47. Here is the question: What did Jan do in Mrs. Gates's room during recess? Choose your answer.

Now listen as I read the rest of the story to you. Listen carefully.

In addition to the hammering, a machine on Mrs. Gates's desk whirred and rumbled. Jan tried to work, but the noise distracted her until Mrs. Gates finally turned off the machine and opened it. "Come and look at this, Jan," she said.

When Jan approached, she saw the machine was full of a muddy liquid, and rocks so slick and black they were almost silver. They made Jan think of the liquid in the bulb at the bottom of a thermometer. "This is a rock tumbler," Mrs. Gates explained, "for polishing rocks. These are obsidian-aren't they beautiful?"

They were. Next, Mrs. Gates showed Jan the plain, gray rock she had been hammering. When the teacher picked it up, it fell open in two hollow chunks, exposing a glittering pink center. "Oh," whispered Jan, "that's incredible!"

"It's a geode," said Mrs. Gates. She gazed at Jan with that serious look, but for the first time, Jan noticed a smile in her eyes.

Excited voices floated in from the hall. "I guess recess is over," said Mrs. Gates, "and I've distracted you from your work. If you'll turn it in before school tomorrow, I won't count it as late."

As Jan left, Brian came up to her, teasing, "I see Mrs. Gates didn't feed you to her snake!"

"You're right, I was being silly," laughed Jan. "She showed me some great stuff. It's like you said; she's not scary, she's just a little different."

Find question 48. Here is the question: What happened after Mrs. Gates showed Jan the geode? Choose your answer.

Find question 49. Here is the question: Which sentence tells what Jan thought about Mrs. Gates at the end of the story? Choose your answer.

Find question 50. Here is the question: Which is the best title for this story? Choose your answer.

Writing Prompt, p. 21

When students are ready, have them turn to page 21. Check to see that all students are on the correct page. Choose *one* writing prompt from the three prompts below. Say: *Now you are going to write a paragraph on this page. Look at the (first, second, or third) paragraph. Read these directions silently while I read them aloud.*

Read the prompt aloud.

Writing Prompts:

Write a story about a time when you changed your mind about a person. Tell what you thought in the beginning and why, and tell what happened to change your mind.

Do you think it's okay to be "a little different?" Write an essay about it, telling why you think as you do.

Think of a craft or art project you know how to do. Write an essay explaining how to do it.

Make sure students understand what they are expected to do.

When you have finished writing, put down your pencils and look at me. You may begin writing now.

End-Year
A Thrilling Ride, p. 3

Have students open their Unit Assessments to page 3. Say: *You will read a story called "A Thrilling Ride" and then answer some questions. Read all four answer choices for each question. Then fill in the circle next to the right answer. When you have finished, put down your pencils and look at me. You may begin now.*

Have students read the story and answer questions 1–10 on pages 4 and 5.

My Business Plan, p. 6

When all the students have finished answering the questions on pages 4–5, have them turn to page 6. Say: *Now you will read a story called "My Business Plan" and then answer some questions. Read all four answer choices for each question. Then fill in the circle next to the right answer. When you have finished, put down your pencils and look at me. You may begin now.*

Have students read the story and answer questions 11–20 on pages 7 and 8.

Rolling Racers, p. 9

When all the students have finished answering the questions on pages 7–8 , have them turn to page 9. Say: *Now you will read a story called "Rolling Racers" and then answer some questions. Read all four answer choices for each question. Then fill in the circle next to the right answer. When you have finished, put down your pencils and look at me. You may begin now.*

Have students read the story and answer questions 21–30 on pages 10 and 11.

A Baseball Legend, p. 12

When all the students have finished answering the questions on pages 10–11, have them turn to page 12. Say: *Now you will read a story called "A Baseball Legend" and then answer some questions. Read all four answer choices for each question. Then fill in the circle next to the right answer. When you have finished, put down your pencils and look at me. You may begin now.*

Have students read the story and answer questions 31–36 on page 13.

Study Skills, pp. 14–19

Have students turn to page 14. Check to see that all students are on the correct page. Say: *Look at the diagram on this page. Take a moment to study it, then use the information in the diagram to answer questions 37–39 on page 15. When you have finished, put down your pencils and look at me. You may begin now.*

Have students turn to page 16. Check to see that all students are on the correct page. Say: *Look at the newspaper article on this page. Take a moment to study the article, then use it to answer questions 40–42 on page 17. When you have finished, put down your pencils and look at me. You may begin now.*

Have students turn to page 18. Check to see that all students are on the correct page. Say: *On this page, you will see several guidelines for conducting an interview. Take a moment to read over the guidelines, then use them to answer questions 43–45 on page 19. When you have finished, put down your pencils and look at me. You may begin now.*

Listening, p. 20

When students are ready, have them turn to page 20 and read the directions at the top of the page. Say: *You are going to hear a story. I will read part of it and ask two questions. Fill in the circle next to the correct answer. Listen carefully. We will begin now.*

September 4
Dear Diary,
What a sad day. The last day of summer. That means that school starts tomorrow. Don't get me wrong; normally I like going back to school at the end of a long summer. I get to see all my friends again, and do fun stuff in class. But this time it's not normal. You see, tomorrow is my first day at the big middle school, and I'm scared to death! It's the first time in my life that I won't be walking down my street to go to Washington Elementary school, where I know everybody and all the teachers, and I know where everything is, and everything is comfortable and familiar. Carver Middle School is huge, and all the way across town. What if I miss the bus? Plus, at Carver, every class is in a different room with a different teacher. I'll have eight teachers and eight classrooms! What if I can't find my classroom? And worst of all, what if none of my friends are in my classes? Every time I think about it, I get butterflies in my stomach.

My mom says not to worry so much. She says everything will go swimmingly. I hope she's right!

That reminds me, the one and only positive thing about going to Carver Middle School is that they have a swim team. Maybe I can make the team.

Now I will stop and ask you two questions. Find question 46 at the top of the page.

Here is question 46: My mom says not to worry so much. She says everything will go swimmingly. What does the word swimmingly *mean? Choose your answer.*

Find question 47. Here is the question: What is the one good thing about Carver Middle School? Choose your answer.

Now listen as I read the rest of the story to you. Listen carefully.

September 5

Dear Diary,

Whew, I made it through the first day of school! And, yes, Mom was right. It went fine. In the morning I walked to the end of my street to wait for the school bus. I was relieved to see my friend April on the bus. We sat together and found out we were in the same math class, our first class of the day. We spent most of the long ride to school in silence. We were too nervous to speak.

When we arrived at the school, we were amazed to see all the people. There were so many students! April and I got off the bus and somehow found our way to math class. Our teacher was really nice. He even took us all on a tour of the school so we would know where we were going for the rest of the day. As we toured, I made a little map so I wouldn't forget. After math, I had plenty of time to make it to my science class. We did experiments on the first day! It was exciting. The time seemed to fly by. At lunch time I found April and met a couple new girls. We had lunch together, and then April and I went to introduce ourselves to the coach of the swim team. She was nice, and the pool looks great.

I guess I worried all summer for nothing. I think it's going to be a good year, especially if I make the swim team. Tryouts are next week. I hope they go as "swimmingly" as today did!

Find question 48. Here is the question: What did the narrator worry about all summer? Choose your answer.

Find question number 49. Here is the question: How did the narrator feel about Carver Middle School at the end of the story? Choose your answer.

Find question number 50. Here is the question: What happened when the narrator boarded the school bus? Choose your answer.

Writing Prompt, p. 21

When students are ready, have them turn to page 21. Check to see that all students are on the correct page. Choose *one* writing prompt from the three prompts below. Say: *Now you are going to write a paragraph on this page. Look at the (first, second, or third) paragraph. Read these directions silently while I read them aloud.*

Read the prompt aloud.

Writing Prompts:

Write an essay about three good things about your school. Include facts and details.

Write an essay comparing yourself to the girl in the story. How would you feel about starting middle school? Why? How did she feel?

Make up a story about someone facing his or her fears and doing something for the first time. What is the person nervous about? How does he or she overcome the fear?

Make sure students understand what they are expected to do.

When you have finished writing, put down your pencils and look at me. You may begin writing now.

McGraw-Hill Reading/Language Arts

Unit Assessments, Grade 5

Answer Sheet

Student Name _____   **Date** _____

Teacher Name _____   **Assessment** _____

1. ⓐ ⓑ ⓒ ⓓ	21. ⓐ ⓑ ⓒ ⓓ	41. ⓐ ⓑ ⓒ ⓓ
2. ⓐ ⓑ ⓒ ⓓ	22. ⓐ ⓑ ⓒ ⓓ	42. ⓐ ⓑ ⓒ ⓓ
3. ⓐ ⓑ ⓒ ⓓ	23. ⓐ ⓑ ⓒ ⓓ	43. ⓐ ⓑ ⓒ ⓓ
4. ⓐ ⓑ ⓒ ⓓ	24. ⓐ ⓑ ⓒ ⓓ	44. ⓐ ⓑ ⓒ ⓓ
5. ⓐ ⓑ ⓒ ⓓ	25. ⓐ ⓑ ⓒ ⓓ	45. ⓐ ⓑ ⓒ ⓓ
6. ⓐ ⓑ ⓒ ⓓ	26. ⓐ ⓑ ⓒ ⓓ	46. ⓐ ⓑ ⓒ ⓓ
7. ⓐ ⓑ ⓒ ⓓ	27. ⓐ ⓑ ⓒ ⓓ	47. ⓐ ⓑ ⓒ ⓓ
8. ⓐ ⓑ ⓒ ⓓ	28. ⓐ ⓑ ⓒ ⓓ	48. ⓐ ⓑ ⓒ ⓓ
9. ⓐ ⓑ ⓒ ⓓ	29. ⓐ ⓑ ⓒ ⓓ	49. ⓐ ⓑ ⓒ ⓓ
10. ⓐ ⓑ ⓒ ⓓ	30. ⓐ ⓑ ⓒ ⓓ	50. ⓐ ⓑ ⓒ ⓓ
11. ⓐ ⓑ ⓒ ⓓ	31. ⓐ ⓑ ⓒ ⓓ	
12. ⓐ ⓑ ⓒ ⓓ	32. ⓐ ⓑ ⓒ ⓓ	
13. ⓐ ⓑ ⓒ ⓓ	33. ⓐ ⓑ ⓒ ⓓ	
14. ⓐ ⓑ ⓒ ⓓ	34. ⓐ ⓑ ⓒ ⓓ	
15. ⓐ ⓑ ⓒ ⓓ	35. ⓐ ⓑ ⓒ ⓓ	
16. ⓐ ⓑ ⓒ ⓓ	36. ⓐ ⓑ ⓒ ⓓ	
17. ⓐ ⓑ ⓒ ⓓ	37. ⓐ ⓑ ⓒ ⓓ	
18. ⓐ ⓑ ⓒ ⓓ	38. ⓐ ⓑ ⓒ ⓓ	
19. ⓐ ⓑ ⓒ ⓓ	39. ⓐ ⓑ ⓒ ⓓ	
20. ⓐ ⓑ ⓒ ⓓ	40. ⓐ ⓑ ⓒ ⓓ	

Comprehension Prompts

Overview

For each unit, there are two forms of the Unit Assessment: the Multiple-Choice form and the Comprehension Prompts. This section of the manual provides directions for administering and scoring the Comprehension Prompts.

Description of Comprehension Prompts

The Comprehension Prompts are designed to provide an alternative method for assessing comprehension through a fully developed written response. There is one Comprehension Prompt for each literature selection in each unit: fiction or non-fiction. Students read each selection and answer a single question by writing a response.

The literature selections in each Unit Assessment are written at a level of difficulty and complexity comparable to those of the reading materials in the unit, and representative of the context in which the strategies and skills have been modeled and applied during instruction. The Comprehension Prompt itself is a question that requires comprehension of the reading selection and the application of strategies and skills taught in the unit.

Directions for Administering the Comprehension Prompts

To administer the Comprehension Prompts, follow these procedures:

1. Hand out copies of the Unit Assessment, which includes the three literature selections.

2. Write the Comprehension Prompts for a particular unit on the chalkboard.

3. When students are ready, read these directions:
   You are going to read three literature selections and answer a single question about each one. To answer each question, you will write one or more paragraphs on a separate piece of paper. Make sure your answer is complete.

4. Have students read the first selection, and then read the first prompt aloud and make sure students understand what they are expected to do. Remind them to write their responses on a separate sheet of paper, with their name and the date at the top of the page.

5. When students have completed their responses for the first prompt, continue in the same way with the second prompt, and then the third.

Comprehension Prompts

PART 3
Comprehension Prompts

■ Unit 1

The Middle of Nowhere:
Story Elements: Character

Imagine you are one of the camp counselors. Write a journal entry describing Ayesha when she first arrives at the camp and again after the first night of star gazing.

The Birthday Present:
Problem and Solution

What is Luke's problem in this story? How is his problem solved? Write at least one paragraph to answer the question.

Treasure Hunters: Cause and Effect

The article mentions Lillian Rade, Michael Miller, and a team that found statues in Romania. What would each do upon finding an old necklace in a field? Write at least one paragraph to answer the question.

■ Unit 2

The Secret Cave:
Make Generalizations

Based on the events in the story, write at least one paragraph giving advice to a friend who is planning to go on a long hike.

Hands Across Time: Fact and Nonfact

Imagine a display of tools from the Stone Age and the Copper Age in a history museum. Use facts from the article to write the descriptive card for the display.

The Golden Cloak: Main Idea

What is "The Golden Cloak" mainly about? Write at least one paragraph to answer the question.

■ Unit 3

Stan Herd, Crop Artist:
Steps in a Process

Write an explanation of how you can make your own crop art in a small garden patch.

Tracy's New Computer:
Sequence of Events

Write a series of short journal entries that Tracy would have written telling what happened from the time she entered the contest to the end of the story.

Johnny Appleseed: Summarize

Why were apples so important to people years ago? Write at least one paragraph to answer the question.

■ Unit 4

Sharks: Important and Unimportant
Information

Do you think sharks are dangerous when you are swimming at the beach? Use important information from the article to support your answer.

Birthday Sky:
Judgments and Decisions

Do you think Julie made the right decision when she got out of bed? Why or why not?

Mrs. Miller's Machine:
Draw Conclusions

Write at least one paragraph describing the skills Mrs. Miller had to have in order to build the time machine.

© McGraw-Hill School Division

■ *Unit 5*

A Room for Two:
Compare and Contrast

Write at least one paragraph comparing the two brothers in the story.

The First Shoes: Make Inferences

Write at least one paragraph that explains why the Great Chief felt ashamed to be the only one with tender feet.

What to Buy Rover?:
Author's Purpose, Point of View

Imagine that you are the author of this article. Write a letter of advice to a friend with a new dog, telling her one thing she should buy and one thing she shouldn't buy.

■ *Unit 6*

Jazz Giant: Cause and Effect

Louis Armstrong spent time in a special school for boys. What effect did this have on his career in music? Write at least one paragraph to answer the question.

Breaking into Broadcasting:
Sequence of Events

Write a letter to a friend from Claire's point of view telling how she broke into broadcasting.

Devin's Decision: Draw Conclusions

Do you agree with the decision Devin made? Write at least one paragraph explaining why or why not.

■ *Mid-Year*

A Fun Way to Remember:
Steps in a Process

Your sister is making a plaster casting of a deer track. She has pulled the mold off of the track, but she can't remember what to do next. Write an explanation of what she should do to complete the project.

Fitting In: Story Elements: Character

How would you describe Derek's sister, Vonda? Write at least one paragraph to answer the question.

The Storage Closet: Make Inferences

Write at least one paragraph telling why Alma asked Mrs. Harwitz if she could sometimes play in the storage closet.

Jacqueline's Gift: Make
Generalizations

Write a one- or two-paragraph description of a typical woman who completed Jacqueline Cochran's WASP program.

■ *End-Year*

A Thrilling Ride:
Judgments and Decisions

Imagine that you are one of the first people to ride the Mauch Chuck Railway ride. Write a letter to the editor of the newspaper telling your opinion of the ride.

My Business Plan: Draw Conclusions

Do you think the narrator's plan will work? Write at least one paragraph explaining your answer.

Rolling Racers: Problem and Solution

What was Manisha's problem in the story? How did she solve it?

A Baseball Legend: Make Inferences

Why do you think Jackie Robinson continued to play for the Brooklyn Dodgers, despite the hatred that he faced? Write at least one paragraph to explain your answer.

Teacher's Notes

Scoring

Overview

This section of the manual provides directions for scoring the assessments. It includes the following:

◆ guidelines for interpreting responses

◆ example items to illustrate responses

◆ procedures for scoring writing samples

◆ examples of student writing to illustrate scores

◆ procedures for scoring tests

Following the directions are the answer keys and scoring charts.

Directions for Scoring the Assessments

For scoring purposes, there are two different parts of each Unit Assessment: comprehension questions and a writing prompt. Each type of question is scored in a different way, as explained in the following paragraphs.

Multiple-Choice Questions

Numbered items (1–25, for example) are multiple-choice questions. These questions measure comprehension in Reading, Vocabulary Strategies, Study Skills, and Listening. Responses to these questions should be marked right or wrong, and the results may be recorded on the Evaluation Charts.

Writing Prompt

The second part of the assessment is the writing prompt. We recommend that you read each studentís response, and score it by using the Primary Trait scoring method, described later in this manual. However, you may also wish to score the writing samples using an analytical approach, so we have included a Writing Analysis Chart for scoring the writing samples analytically.

Scoring methods and criteria for the types of questions in both parts of the Unit Assessments are explained in the following pages, with example student responses to illustrate how to interpret answers to Writing Prompts. Forms for scoring and evaluating assessments are provided at the end of this section. These forms may be copied for your use.

Scoring The Writing Samples

The writing task in each assessment presents a writing prompt and requires students to produce writing samples. Each writing prompt requires a certain kind of writing (description, how-to, narrative story, etc.), and the scoring criteria reflects differences in writing tasks.

Writing samples may be scored and evaluated in a number of different ways. Two basic approaches are explained below.

Primary trait scoring relies on the concept that every piece of writing should possess or satisfy certain traits or characteristics. The reader evaluates the overall quality of the writing in relation to one or more specified traits or characteristics. For example, the primary trait might be "The student tells an entertaining story," or "The student describes a place with vivid adjectives." Again, the reader assigns a score of 1, 2, 3, or 4 to each piece of writing.

This method is relatively fast and easy to use. The second method, *analytical scoring*, is somewhat more involved. Analytical scoring relies on evaluation of the many aspects of a piece of writing, such as main idea, use of details, grammar, capitalization, and spelling. The reader marks errors and problems in the writing and derives a score by counting the number of errors.

In this program, instruction in writing emphasizes the ability to produce different types of writing and to write in different modes: descriptive, narrative, persuasive, and so on. Each type of writing and each mode has different requirements and characteristics, so the method of scoring studentsí writing should also be based on sets of criteria.

Scoring Procedure

To score the writing sample, review the criteria listed in the scoring rubric. These criteria apply to all writing samples.

Sample Responses

The next few pages provide actual student writing in response to a sample writing prompt.

These samples illustrate the range of quality in writing samples rated from 1 to 4, and they may be helpful to you in determining the standards of good writing expected in your class. Please keep in mind, however, that these samples were written by students in the first few weeks of Grade 5. They will be most appropriate for comparisons at the beginning of the year.

Writing Prompt

What is a new baby like? Imagine a new baby. Write a description of it.

> I have a little sister and she live in Alantia she say Mom and she laigh she smell very good hername is Ranylee and my old sister Kim. half-sister have a little boy and having a girl Sept. 30 it is due.
>
> My cousin Nicole have a little girl in August she live in Akron ohio her baby is very cute looking.

Sample 1

Score: 1—Unsatisfactory

Sample 1 comments:

Ideas and Content—this sample does not respond to the task. Instead of describing a baby, it gives information about the writer's family and some of the babies he knows.

Organization—an attempt has been made to divide the sample into paragraphs, but there is no logic to the division.

Voice—the writer does not try to convey a personal style.

Word Choice—the words "cute looking" are too vague to fully describe a baby.

Sentence Fluency—the writer doesn't seem to have a grasp on basic sentence structure.

Conventions—mistakes in grammar, mechanics, and usage detract from clarity and meaning.

> I think a newborn baby looks like the size of someones hand. A newborn baby feels soft and as list as a feather. They move as if they were real happy. They do cry alot. Newborn babies smell bad I don't know why but they do
>
> That's how I fell about a babies actions.

Sample 2

Score: 2—Fair

Sample 2 comments:

Ideas and Content—this sample attempts to describe a baby, but is somewhat underdeveloped.

Organization—the writer has trouble tying ideas together.

Voice—the writer does not connect with the audience.

Word Choice—the writer does not choose words that create a striking picture for the reader.

Sentence Fluency—the sentences are understandable, but choppy.

Conventions—mistakes in grammar, mechanics, and usage don't really detract from meaning.

© McGraw-Hill School Division

> Newborn babies are so beautiful. They feel so soft and cuddly. Newborns are so cute. Most of the time they cry, but sometimes they make cute little noises. They move their arms and legs. Sometimes they make fists which makes them look so adorable. After they drink a bottle they usually smell like baby formula, but otherwise they smell like baby powder.
>
> It feels so wonderful to hold a little baby in your arms. It feels so great that you never want to let go. If you have a baby sister or brother you are so lucky.

Sample 3

Score: 3—Good

Sample 3 comments:

Ideas and Content—the writer presents a focused, clear description.

Organization—the description is easy to follow; the ideas are smoothly connected.

Voice—the writer is involved with the topic.

Word Choice—the writer chooses a variety of words that create an accurate picture for the reader.

Sentence Fluency—sentences are carefully constructed and easy-to-follow.

Conventions—errors in spelling and usage do not interfere with understanding.

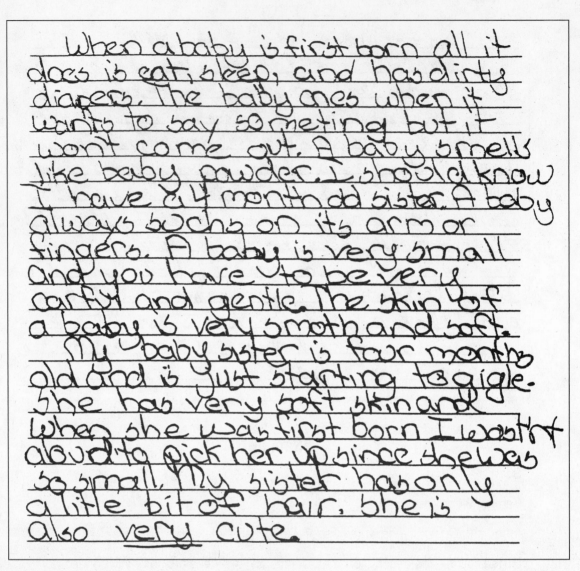

When a baby is first born all it does is eat, sleep, and has dirty diapers. The baby cries when it wants to say someting but it won't come out. A baby smells like baby powder. I should know I have a 4 month old sister. A baby always sucks on its arm or fingers. A baby is very small and you have to be very carful and gentle. The skin of a baby is very smoth and soft.

My baby sister is four months old and is just starting to gigle. She has very soft skin and when she was first born I wasn't aloud to pick her up since she was so small. My sister has only a litle bit of hair. She is also very cute.

Sample 4

Score: 4—Excellent

Sample 4 comments:

Ideas and Content—this sample focuses on the purpose of the task, with many details.

Organization—presents descriptive details in a well-organized way.

Voice—this sample shows deep involvement with the topic. The writer's personal message is skillfully linked to the purpose and audience.

Word Choice—the writer makes sophisticated choices that create a striking picture.

Sentence Fluency—some sentences are choppy, but overall description flows with a smooth rhythm.

Conventions—mistakes in grammar, mechanics, and usage do not detract from clarity and meaning.

Personal Narrative

Scoring Rubric: 6-Trait Writing

4. EXCELLENT	3. GOOD	2. FAIR	1. UNSATISFACTORY
Ideas & Content • creates an entertaining, vividly-detailed story; shares fresh insights about the topic	**Ideas & Content** • crafts a clear, focused piece of writing; details help clarify important ideas and insights; holds the reader's attention	**Ideas & Content** • attempts to address the topic, but may not elaborate thoroughly; may lose control of the narrative line; details may be general, or unrelated to the story	**Ideas & Content** • does not tell a personal story; writer may go off in several directions, without a sense of purpose
Organization • unfolds a carefully-organized narrative, in a sequence that moves the reader smoothly through the events	**Organization** • shows a well-planned narrative strategy; story is easy to follow; ideas are evenly tied together	**Organization** • may not have clear story structure, or may have trouble tying ideas together; reader may be confused by details	**Organization** • writing is hard to follow; story sequence is disorganized or incomplete; ideas and details are not tied together
Voice • conveys an original, reflective message that speaks directly to the reader; is deeply involved with the topic	**Voice** • makes a strong effort to share an authentic personal message; attempts to explore a range of feelings; style connects with the story purpose	**Voice** • tells a story, but in a predictable way; gets the basic message across, but does not seem involved with the topic or audience	**Voice** • is not involved in sharing an experience with a reader; does not focus on anything of personal importance or interest; writing is flat and lifeless
Word Choice • uses sophisticated figurative and everyday language in an imaginative, natural way, to paint a memorable picture and bring the story to life	**Word Choice** • carefully selects words that fit the story and bring the main events to life; experiments with some new words	**Word Choice** • may not use words that convey specific feelings or images; words are overused, or may not fit; some words detract from the story's meaning or impact	**Word Choice** • has a hard time finding the right words; may make run-on lists of disconnected words and phrases; some vocabulary detracts from the meaning
Sentence Fluency • creative, effective sentences flow in a smooth rhythm; dialogue, if used, sounds natural and strengthens the story	**Sentence Fluency** • crafts fluid, easy-to-follow sentences; may effectively use fragments and/or dialogue to enhance the story	**Sentence Fluency** • may have trouble with complicated structures; sentences may be, rambling or awkward; writing is hard to read aloud	**Sentence Fluency** • sentences are incomplete, rambling, or confusing; may have trouble understanding how words and sentences fit together
Conventions • is skilled in most writing conventions; proper use of the rules of English enhances clarity and narrative style	**Conventions** • spelling, capitalization, punctuation and usage are mostly correct; minor errors don't interfere with following the story; some editing may be needed	**Conventions** • makes frequent, noticeable mistakes which interfere with a smooth reading of the story; extensive editing is needed	**Conventions** • makes errors in spelling, word choice, punctuation and usage; sentence structures may be confused; few connections made between ideas

0: This piece is either blank, or fails to respond to the writing task. The topic is not addressed, or the student simply paraphrases the prompt. The response may be illegible or incoherent.

Persuasive Writing

Scoring Rubric: 6-Trait Writing

4. EXCELLENT

Ideas & Content
- crafts a compelling editorial, with extensive supporting details; shares fresh insights and observations

Organization
- keen strategy moves the reader logically through the text, well-placed ideas and details strengthen the argument

Voice
- conveys a strong, authentic personal message, capable of influencing a reader's opinion; deep involvement with the topic enlivens the content; reaches out to an audience

Word Choice
- imaginative use of precise, sophisticated word choices helps to create a powerfully-convincing tone

Sentence Fluency
- varied, effective sentences flow naturally; uses both simple and complex sentences creatively; varied beginnings, lengths, and patterns add appeal

Conventions
- proper use of the rules of English enhances clarity, style, and cohesion of the argument; editing is largely unnecessary

3. GOOD

Ideas & Content
- crafts a solid, well-thought-out editorial; details show knowledge of the topic; may make some new connections about the topic

Organization
- audience can follow the writer's logic from beginning to end; details fit and build on each other

Voice
- clearly shows who is behind the words; personal style matches the purpose; reaches out to convince the reader

Word Choice
- uses a range of precise words to state opinions, facts, and observations; may experiment with new words, or use everyday words to share ideas in a fresh way

Sentence Fluency
- crafts careful sentences that make sense, and are easy to read and understand; sentence lengths and patterns vary, and fit together well

Conventions
- uses most conventions correctly; some editing may be needed; errors are few and don't make the paper hard to understand

2. FAIR

Ideas & Content
- attempts to craft a persuasive editorial, but may not offer clear or thorough facts and details

Organization
- has trouble consistently ordering facts and ideas; states a main idea, but may lose control of the persuasive form; poorly-placed details

Voice
- gives some hint of who is behind the words; writer may seem personally uninvolved with the topic

Word Choice
- gets the main idea across in a predictable way; experiments with few new words; may not choose strong enough words to influence a reader

Sentence Fluency
- sentences are understandable, but choppy, rambling, or awkward; hard to follow or read aloud

Conventions
- makes frequent noticeable mistakes which prevent a smooth reading of the text; extensive need for editing

1. UNSATISFACTORY

Ideas & Content
- does not successfully argue a position; it is hard to tell what the writer thinks or feels about the topic

Organization
- extreme lack of structure makes the text hard to follow; ideas, facts, and details are not connected, and may not fit the purpose

Voice
- writer does not connect with the topic; is not involved in sharing ideas with a reader

Word Choice
- does not use words that express an opinion or attempt to convince a reader; words do not fit, or are overused

Sentence Fluency
- uses choppy, rambling, or confusing sentences; does not understand how words and sentences fit together; and is hard to read aloud

Conventions
- has extensive errors in spelling, word choice, punctuation and usage; some parts are impossible to read or understand

0: This piece is either blank, or fails to respond to the writing task. The topic is not addressed, or the student simply paraphrases the prompt. The response may be illegible or incoherent.

Explanatory Writing

Scoring Rubric: 6-Trait Writing

4. EXCELLENT

Ideas & Content
- presents a focused, interesting how-to project, with an elaborate set of details

Organization
- easy-to-follow time sequence leads the reader logically through each stage; steps and details clarify the process

Voice
- exceptionally strong personal touch speaks to the reader, and enlivens the project content; cleverly connects the writing style to the purpose

Word Choice
- thoughtful, imaginative use of precise language creates a colorful picture of the how-to process

Sentence Fluency
- varied, well-crafted sentences flow with a natural rhythm; fragments, if used, add appeal to the explanation

Conventions
- proper use of the rules of English enhances clarity and personal style; editing largely unnecessary

3. GOOD

Ideas & Content
- presents a focused, interesting project, with details that clearly describe the main idea

Organization
- logical sequence helps a reader to follow the process from beginning to end; details are placed to make sense, and help to clarify each ste

Voice
- genuine personal style reaches out to the reader, and shows who is behind the writing

Word Choice
- uses a variety of words that clarify the process; experiments with new words, or uses everyday words to present ideas in a fresh way

Sentence Fluency
- carefully-devised sentences are easy to read and follow; beginnings, lengths, and patterns vary and fit together

Conventions
- uses a variety of conventions correctly; some editing may be needed; errors are few

2. FAIR

Ideas & Content
- has some control of a how-to explanation, but may not offer clear or thorough details

Organization
- tries to structure a logical process, but may have trouble keeping ideas in order; reader may be confused by poorly-placed steps and details

Voice
- communicates ideas in an ordinary way; gives some hint of who is behind the words; may not show involvement with an audience, or with the topic project

Word Choice
- explores few new words; does not use accurate or colorful words to create a clear picture of the how-to process

Sentence Fluency
- may have trouble with more complex sentences; sentences are understandable, but may be choppy, rambling, or awkward.

Conventions
- makes frequent mistakes which may interfere with a smooth reading

1. UNSATISFACTORY

Ideas & Content
- does not explain a how-to process; writing may go off in several directions, without a sense of purpose

Organization
- does not present a clear structure; ideas are disconnected; no clear beginning or ending

Voice
- is not involved in the topic; lacks awareness of a reader

Word Choice
- does not use words that describe a process; some words may detract from the meaning of the text

Sentence Fluency
- constructs incomplete, rambling, or confusing sentences, which may interfere with following a process; does not understand how words and sentences fit together

Conventions
- makes repeated errors in spelling, word choice, punctuation and usage; sentence structures may be confused

0: This piece is either blank, or fails to respond to the writing task. The topic is not addressed, or the student simply paraphrases the prompt. The response may be illegible or incoherent.

Expository Writing

Scoring Rubric: 6-Trait Writing

4. EXCELLENT	3. GOOD	2. FAIR	1. UNSATISFACTORY
Ideas & Content • devises a focused, thoroughly-detailed report; makes fresh, accurate connections between key facts and observations.	**Ideas & Content** • presents a clear, carefully-researched report; details show knowledge of the topic; shares accurate information and observations	**Ideas & Content** • details and ideas are vague, undeveloped, or do not fit; writer may make predictable observations about the topic	**Ideas & Content** • does not successfully report on the topic; writer may not grasp the purpose, or may offer very limited facts and ideas
Organization • careful structure moves the reader logically through the text; information and paragraphs are smoothly tied together	**Organization** • logic is easy to follow; details fit, and reinforce facts; ideas, paragraphs, and sentences are connected	**Organization** • tries to shape a report, but may have trouble ordering facts and comments; reader may be confused by vague or disconnected details	**Organization** • logic is hard to follow; ideas and details are disconnected, or out of order; no sense of a clear beginning or ending
Voice • shows deep involvement with the topic; distinct style enlivens the content; message is linked to the purpose and audience	**Voice** • is involved with the topic; devises a style that relates to the topic and audience	**Voice** • may not connect a distinct personal message or style to the facts; is not very involved with the topic, or an audience	**Voice** • is not involved in the topic; does not try to convey a personal style or address ideas to an audience
Word Choice • effective use of precise, colorful language makes the message clear and interesting; vocabulary is vivid and diverse, but natural	**Word Choice** • uses a variety of words to create an accurate picture for the reader; experiments with challenging words, or uses everyday words in a fresh way	**Word Choice** • gets the message across, in an average way; experiments with few new words; some words may not fit the topic	**Word Choice** • chooses words that don't fit, or which confuse reader; no new words are attempted; familiar words are overused
Sentence Fluency • crafts fluid simple and complex sentences; varied beginnings, lengths, and patterns add interest; effective use of sentences	**Sentence Fluency** • crafts simple and complex sentences that are easy to read aloud; lengths and patterns vary, and fit together well	**Sentence Fluency** • most sentences are understandable, but may be choppy, monotonous, or run-on; writer may have trouble with more complex sentences	**Sentence Fluency** • constructs incomplete or confusing sentences; does not grasp how words and sentences fit together; writing is hard to read aloud
Conventions • correctly uses common and proper nouns; proper use of the rules of English enhances clarity, style, and cohesion of ideas; editing is largely unnecessary	**Conventions** • uses a variety of conventions correctly; some editing may be needed; errors are few and don't make the paper hard to understand	**Conventions** • makes noticeable mistakes that prevent a smooth reading of the text; extensive need for editing and revision	**Conventions** • makes repeated errors in word choice, punctuation and usage; spelling errors make it hard to guess what words are meant

0: This piece is either blank, or fails to respond to the writing task. The topic is not addressed, or the student simply paraphrases the prompt. The response may be illegible or incoherent.

Writing That Compares

Scoring Rubric: 6-Trait Writing

4. EXCELLENT

Ideas & Content
- skillfully compares two things; carefully-selected details clarify each comparison point

Organization
- careful strategy moves the reader smoothly through each point; well-placed observations and details strengthen the logic

Voice
- deep involvement with the topic enlivens the content; writer reaches out to share ideas with an audience

Word Choice
- makes imaginative use of strong, advanced vocabulary to describe explicit differences and similarities

Sentence Fluency
- varied sentences flow naturally; uses both simple and complex sentences; varied beginnings, lengths, and patterns add appeal

Conventions
- proper use of the rules of English enhances clarity and cohesion of the comparisons; editing is largely unnecessary

3. GOOD

Ideas & Content
- crafts a solid, well-thought-out comparison; details bring the main idea into focus; may share some new insights about their experiences

Organization
- presents a capable, solid strategy; reader can follow the logic from beginning to end; details fit and build on each other

Voice
- shows who is behind the words; personal style matches the purpose; reaches out to the reader

Word Choice
- uses a range of precise words to present facts and observations; explores some challenging words, or uses everyday words to state ideas in a fresh way

Sentence Fluency
- crafts careful sentences that make sense, and are easy to read and understand; sentence lengths and patterns vary, and fit together well

Conventions
- uses most conventions correctly; some editing may be needed; errors are few

2. FAIR

Ideas & Content
- has some control of the comparison task, but may offer limited or unclear facts and details; makes obvious connections about the topic

Organization
- tries to build a structure, but has trouble sequencing ideas; may not present distinct comparison categories; poorly-placed facts and details

Voice
- communicates a main idea, with some hint of who is behind the words; writer may seem personally uninvolved with the topic and an audience

Word Choice
- gets the argument across, but experiments with few new words

Sentence Fluency
- sentences are understandable, but may be choppy, rambling, or awkward; writing is difficult to follow or read aloud

Conventions
- frequent noticeable mistakes prevent an even reading of the text; extensive need for editing and revision

1. UNSATISFACTORY

Ideas & Content
- does not successfully compare two things; it is hard to tell what the writer intended to say

Organization
- extreme lack of structure makes the text hard to follow; ideas, facts, and details are disconnected, out of order

Voice
- does not connect with the topic; is not involved in sharing ideas with a reader

Word Choice
- does not use words that show differences or similarities; some words may detract from the purpose to compare; words do not fit, or are overused

Sentence Fluency
- uses choppy, rambling, or confusing sentences; does not understand how words and sentences fit together; writing doesn't follow natural sentence patterns, and is hard to read aloud

Conventions
- has repeated errors in spelling, word choice, punctuation and usage; some parts are impossible to read

0: This piece is either blank, or fails to respond to the writing task. The topic is not addressed, or the student simply paraphrases the prompt. The response may be illegible or incoherent.

Writing a Story

Scoring Rubric: 6-Trait Writing

4. EXCELLENT

Ideas & Content
- creates an entertaining, richly-detailed story; characters, setting, and events are skillfully developed

Organization
- unfolds a consistent, carefully-planned narrative; sequence moves the reader smoothly through events

Voice
- shows originality, liveliness, and a strong personal message that speaks directly to the reader

Word Choice
- imaginative use of figurative and everyday words brings the story to life; sophisticated vocabulary creates a striking picture of individual characters

Sentence Fluency
- crafts creative, effective sentences that flow in a smooth rhythm; dialogue, if used, sounds natural and animates the story

Conventions
- shows strong skills in a wide range of writing conventions; proper use of the rules of English enhances clarity and narrative style

3. GOOD

Ideas & Content
- presents a focused, interesting story with characters, setting, and events

Organization
- has a carefully-planned narrative strategy; story is easy to follow, through beginning, middle, and end; ideas are evenly connected

Voice
- makes a strong effort to share an authentic personal message that reaches out to an audience

Word Choice
- has overall clarity of expression; effective control of both new and everyday words

Sentence Fluency
- crafts careful, easy-to-follow sentences; may effectively use fragments and/or dialogue to strengthen and enhance the story

Conventions
- makes some errors in spelling, capitalization, punctuation or usage, but these do not interfere with understanding the story; some editing may be needed

2. FAIR

Ideas & Content
- attempts to write a story, may not elaborate adequately; may lose control of the narrative after a good beginning

Organization
- may not craft a clear story structure, or may have trouble tying ideas and events together; story line may be vague or incomplete

Voice
- may get the basic story across, without a sense of involvement of reaching out to an audience; writing is flat and lifeless

Word Choice
- does not explore words that express clear ideas or feelings; may not choose words that create memorable pictures for the reader

Sentence Fluency
- may have trouble with complex sentences; sentences are understandable, but may be choppy, rambling, or awkward

Conventions
- makes enough noticeable mistakes which may interfere with a smooth reading of the story

1. UNSATISFACTORY

Ideas & Content
- may not understand how to tell a story; narrative may go off in several directions, without a sense of purpose

Organization
- shows extreme lack of organization that interferes with understanding the text; sequence of events may be disorganized or incomplete

Voice
- does not attempt to make sense, share ideas, or connect with a reader

Word Choice
- does not choose words that convey clear feelings or images; some word choices may detract from the meaning of the story

Sentence Fluency
- constructs incomplete, rambling, or confusing sentences; may have trouble understanding how words, ideas, and sentences fit together

Conventions
- makes repeated errors in spelling, word choice, punctuation and usage; errors prevent an even reading of the text

0: This piece is either blank, or fails to respond to the writing task. The topic is not addressed, or the student simply paraphrases the prompt. The response may be illegible or incoherent.

Scoring the Assessments

Analytical Writing Scoring Procedures

The **Writing Analysis Chart** may be used to score writing samples analytically, based on general criteria. The **Grammar, Mechanics, and Usage Skills** chart lists the skills taught in each unit.

PART 4
Scoring

Writing Analysis Chart

Student Name _____ **Date** _____

Assessment _____ **Grade 5** _____ **Unit** _____

Directions: Analyze the student's writing by scoring the work on each of the three major categories listed below. Compare the student's writing with the quality of writing expected from students at this level of instruction. Then assign a score of 1–4 on each category. Scoring: 1 = Poor; 2 = Fair; 3 = Good; 4 = Excellent

Characteristics of Student's Writing	Rating			
Focus/Purpose	1	2	3	4
Establishes and maintains focus				
Meets purpose of writing task				
Shows awareness of audience				
Content/Organization	1	2	3	4
Has an appropriate opening and closing				
Includes information and details specific to focus and topic				
Shows development of ideas				
Organizes content in logical order or sequence				
Paragraphs deal with one subject; sentences relate to topic of paragraph				
Uses appropriate transitions				
Grammar, Mechanics, and Usage	1	2	3	4
Uses proper grammar and usage				
Uses appropriate word choice				
Uses proper sentence construction				
Uses correct punctuation				
Uses correct capitalization				
Uses correct spelling				

Notes and Comments

Grammar, Mechanics, and Usage Skills

This chart shows the specific writing, grammar, mechanics, and usage skills taught in Grade 5, Units 1–6.

WRITING	GRAMMAR, MECHANICS, & USAGE

Unit 1: Personal Narrative
 	
Creates an entertaining, vividly-detailed story about a person; shares fresh insights about learning from an experience.
 	
Unfolds a carefully-organized narrative, in a sequence that moves the reader smoothly through the events; ideas, sentences, and paragraphs are skillfully tied together.
 	
Conveys an original, reflective message that speaks directly to the reader; is deeply involved with the topic; expresses a wide range of feelings about making wise decisions.
 	
Uses sophisticated figurative and everyday language in an imaginative, natural way, to paint a memorable picture and bring the story to life.
	Sentences
	    Sentence Punctuation
	Subjects
	    Letter punctuation
	Sentence Combining
	    Sentence Punctuation
	More Sentence Combining
	    Quotations
	Run-on Sentences
	    Sentence Punctuation

Unit 2: Persuasive Writing
 	
Crafts a compelling editorial, with extensive supporting details; shares fresh insights and observations about reaching personal goals.
 	
Keen strategy moves the reader logically and evenly through the text, from beginning to end; well-placed ideas and details strengthen the argument.
 	
Conveys a strong, authentic personal message, capable of influencing a reader's opinion; deep involvement with the topic enlivens the content; reaches out to an audience.
 	
Imaginative use of precise, sophisticated word choices helps to create a powerfully-convincing tone.
	Common and Proper Nouns
	    Abbreviations
	Singular and Plural Nouns
	    Titles
	Plural Spellings
	    Commas in a Series
	Possessive Nouns
	    Capitalization
	Plurals and Possessives
	    Plural and Possessive Nouns

Unit 3: Explanatory Writing
 	
Devises a focused, thoroughly-detailed report on a familiar natural environment; makes fresh, accurate connections between key facts and observations.
 	
Careful, effective structure moves the reader logically through the text; information and paragraphs are smoothly tied together; inviting beginning and satisfying conclusion.
 	
Shows deep involvement with the topic; distinct style enlivens the factual content; personal message is skillfully linked to the purpose and audience.
 	
Effective use of precise, colorful language makes the message clear and interesting; vocabulary is vivid and diverse, but natural.
	Action Verbs
	    Commas in a Series
	Verb Tenses
	    Spelling Changes
	Main and Helping Verbs
	    Contractions
	Linking Verbs
	    Abbreviations
	Irregular Verbs
	    Using Commas

WRITING	GRAMMAR, MECHANICS, & USAGE
Unit 4: Expository Writing Presents a focused, interesting group how-to process, with an elaborate set of details. Clear, easy-to-follow time sequence leads the reader logically through the process; steps and details are carefully placed to move the process forward. Exceptionally strong personal style speaks directly to the reader, and enlivens the project content. Thoughtful, imaginative use of accurate, specific language creates a vivid picture of the how-to process.	**Adjectives** 　**Proper Adjectives** **Articles** 　**Quotations** **Adjectives That Compare** 　**Letter Punctuation** **Comparing with _More_ and _Most_** 　**Using _More_ and _Most_** **Comparing with _Good_** 　**Proper Adjectives**
Unit 5: Writing That Compares Skillfully compares two personal experiences; carefully-selected details clarify each comparison point; fresh insights add interest to the facts. Careful strategy moves the reader smoothly through each point, from beginning to end; well-placed observations and details strengthen the logic. Originality and deep involvement with the topic enlivens the content; writer reaches out to share ideas with an audience. Makes imaginative use of strong, advanced vocabulary to describe explicit differences and similarities.	**Pronouns** 　**Contractions** **Subject Pronouns** 　**Using _I_ and _me_** **Pronoun-Verb Agreement** 　**Capitalization** **Possessive Pronouns** 　**Using Hyphens** **Pronouns and Homophones** 　**Apostrophes and Possessives**
Unit 6: Write a Story Creates an entertaining, richly-detailed story about overcoming an obstacle; characters, setting, and events are skillfully developed. Unfolds a consistent, carefully-planned narrative; sequence moves the reader smoothly through events; inviting beginning and satisfying ending. Shows originality, liveliness, and a strong personal message that speaks directly to the reader; explores a wide range of emotions. Imaginative use of figurative and everyday words brings the story to life; sophisticated vocabulary creates a striking picture of individual characters who overcome an obstacle.	**Adverbs** 　**Using _Good_ and _Well_** **Adverbs That Compare** 　**_More_ and _Most_** **Avoiding Double Negatives** 　**Avoiding Double Negatives** **Prepositions** **Combining with Adjectives and Adverbs**

Scoring Procedure Continued

This section of the manual describes procedures for scoring the Unit Assessments. It includes:

◆ Answer Keys

◆ Evaluation Form

◆ Class Summary Chart

◆ Class Record Chart

The **Evaluation Form** may be used at any time during the school year to record and evaluate information about students' knowledge and use of reading strategies, interests, attitudes, and appreciation. The **Unit Assessment Class Summary** may be used to record scores for the entire class on each Unit Assessment. **The Class Record** may be used to record all students' scores on all the Unit Assessments given during the year.

Student Scoring   Students can learn quite a lot by reviewing the answers and scoring their own assessments. The scoring activity could become a group discussion about why certain answers are right or wrong—which then becomes a discussion of the literature selections and other activities. This approach to scoring strengthens the cooperative nature of assessment in this program and will help to improve students' perceptions in their own self-assessments.

If you wish to use the "student option" to score these assessments, follow the procedure described on the next page. Read the scoring directions to the students and work through the answers. You may wish to check studentsí work after they pass in their tests and charts.

The score for each category may be recorded on the Evaluation Chart for the Unit Assessment. In addition to these criteria, the specific skills taught in each unit are listed in the Grammar, Mechanics, and Usage Skills chart. Use these specific skills to help determine the expected quality of studentís writing in a given unit.

Using the Evaluation Chart found at the end of each Unit Assessment, Mid-Year Assessment, and End-Year Assessment, score the assessments by following this procedure:

1. Mark each incorrect item on the Evaluation Chart by placing an X over the item number.

2. Count the number of correct responses for each subtest and write the number in the "Student Score" box.

3. Add the subtest scores (number correct) to determine the total test score.

4. If you wish to compute percentage scores for each domain or the total test, you may write the percentage scores in the appropriate boxes.

Find Percentage Scores   The Evaluation Chart provides a score for each domain and a total score for each assessment. The score from the chart is expressed in terms of the number of items answered correctly divided by the total number of items in the domain or total test (for example, 12/16). A student who answers 12 to 16 items correctly has achieved a percentage score of 75% (12 divided by 16 = .75, or 75%).

To convert each domain score or total test score to a percentage, you may use the Conversion Table inside the back cover of this manual. To use this table, find the number of items answered correctly in the column on the left. Then find the column showing the total number of items at the top. Where the row and column meet is the percentage score.

Example: A student scores 12 out of 16 correct in Comprehension. Find the number 12 in the left-hand column. Then go across the row to the "16" column. The number where the row and the column meet is the student's percentage score: 75%.

Passing Scores

The Unit Assessments are criterion-referenced tests, and this kind of test is generally scored in relation to a criterion score, or cut score. A student who achieves the criterion score or higher has passed the test; a student who scores below the criterion score does not pass.

The primary focus of assessments in this program is to measure student progress toward achieving the goals and outcomes taught at each level. From this viewpoint, a student's percentage score on the Unit Assessment implies a range of progress. The Evaluation Chart is designed as an aid in determining and record the student's range of progress: for example, the student may score in the 70–79% range. The most important criterion may not be the studentís score on a single test, but the progression of scores on the Unit Assessments from the beginning of the year to the end.

The Unit Assessments are designed for scoring by domain, or subtest, and by total test. If you choose to apply a criterion score in judging the studentís progress, we would recommend a criterion score in the 60–70% range. In other words, a student should attain a score of at least 60–70% correct on the total test to achieve a passing score. In Writing, the criterion score would be a 2 or better (on the 4-point scale).

You may wish to set higher or lower criterion scores based on the range of student scores in your classroom or the length of time using the program.

Students Acquiring English   In all aspects of scoring and evaluating assessments, special considerations may be needed for students acquiring English. The range of progress achieved by each student, from one assessment to another, should be considered more important than specific passing scores.

© McGraw-Hill School Division

Interpreting and Using Results

In McGraw-Hill Reading, assessment information for each student should be derived from a variety of sources in the student's portfolio: for example, results on the Unit Assessment, writing samples, performance tasks, classroom observations, and self-assessments. The student's performance should not be evaluated on the basis of one test or one activity.

Results on the Unit Assessments may be most useful in providing objective data to consider along with other kinds of information. These results may be used as one of several sources of information for evaluating student performance. In all cases, results should be interpreted in relation to the purpose of the assessment and the program goals and outcomes for each level.

Placement Decisions   In some cases, you may feel that one or more students should begin the year at a higher or lower level in the instructional program. For these students, you may wish to collect additional assessment information. If so, try this approach:

1. Review the student's past performance: for example, portfolio records from the previous year.

2. Talk with the student about the Evaluation Forms for Reading Strategies, Interests, Attitudes, and Appreciation. Talking with the student may reveal information that is helpful in interpreting test results.

3. Administer the **Individual Reading Inventory and Running Record** in the Diagnostic Placement/Evaluation Book, which is designed to help you collect more detailed information about each student. Results can be used to determine the best instructional level for the student.

The assessment information gathered from various sources can be used to determine instructional placement and to develop an instructional plan that emphasizes specific areas for each student.

Planning for Reteaching

The **Unit Assessments, Mid-Year Assessment,** and **End-Year Assessment** are designed to measure student progress. Results from these assessments may be used to determine needs for reteaching. However, it bears repeating that results from the Unit Assessments should not be used as the sole source of information for evaluating students. The portfolio is designed to help provide a comprehensive profile of each student; assessment should be continuous and ongoing throughout the unit and throughout the school year.

The need for reteaching should be determined on the basis of *progress*: Has the student shown adequate progress in reteaching the goals stated for the unit? Performing poorly on one activity or missing a few questions on specific skills should not automatically be interpreted as failing to make adequate progress. For students who do not seem to be making adequate progress, here are some suggestions.

◆ You may want to do some reteaching with individual students by going back to the literature in the current unit.

Reteaching needs may also be based on the instructional notion that students can learn thinking strategies which can then be selected and applied when needed. The strategies do not change significantly from one unit to another, but the student learns more strategies and gets better at using them. Instruction is a recursive process, so strategies that the student has not learned well in this unit will be taught again in later units.

◆ You may want to note areas in which students are having difficulties and emphasize these areas in the next unit by providing additional practice or individualized guidance.

Given these instructional principles, the most effective way to provide additional instruction for students is to teach strategies in alternative contexts. In all of the instructional materials, strategies are derived from the literature and are closely integrated within each domain (Reading, Writing, and so on).

This program provides a number of different theme-related materials in each unit, which may be used as alternative contexts for teaching strategies in different ways or offering opportunities for additional practice. For each unit, refer to the Alternative Contexts for Reteaching Skills and Strategies in Part 5 of this manual for specific activities suitable for reteaching skills and strategies.

◆ You may use any of these materials as alternative contexts for teaching in each unit:

Skills Minilessons

Prevention/Intervention

Reteaching Blackline Masters

Alternate Teaching Strategies

Language Support

Unit Writing Process Lessons

Meeting Individual Needs for Writing

◆ You may use another form of the Progress Assessment (Comprehension Prompt or Written Response form) for individual guided instruction or follow-up assessment.

Results from the Unit Assessments should be incorporated into the portfolio as part of the comprehensive profile of each student.

ANSWER KEY

Unit 1	Unit 2	Unit 3	Unit 4	Unit 5
1. c	1. a	1. a	1. a	1. a
2. a	2. c	2. b	2. b	2. c
3. d	3. a	3. d	3. a	3. c
4. b	4. b	4. a	4. a	4. b
5. a	5. a	5. c	5. a	5. b
6. d	6. b	6. d	6. a	6. a
7. a	7. a	7. b	7. a	7. a
8. b	8. d	8. a	8. a	8. a
9. c	9. a	9. a	9. d	9. b
10. a	10. d	10. b	10. b	10. d
11. d	11. c	11. a	11. a	11. b
12. a	12. a	12. c	12. b	12. a
13. a	13. b	13. c	13. b	13. a
14. b	14. a	14. a	14. d	14. a
15. a	15. c	15. b	15. b	15. b
16. b	16. b	16. c	16. a	16. d
17. c	17. b	17. d	17. b	17. a
18. b	18. a	18. a	18. a	18. c
19. d	19. b	19. c	19. c	19. c
20. c	20. d	20. b	20. b	20. a
21. c	21. b	21. b	21. b	21. c
22. a	22. c	22. a	22. a	22. a
23. b	23. b	23. a	23. b	23. b
24. a	24. b	24. c	24. b	24. c
25. c	25. b	25. d	25. c	25. c

Unit 6	Mid-Year	26. a	End Year	26. b
1. c	1. d	27. c	1. d	27. d
2. a	2. a	28. a	2. c	28. d
3. a	3. c	29. b	3. c	29. b
4. b	4. b	30. c	4. a	30. d
5. b	5. d	31. b	5. d	31. c
6. c	6. d	32. a	6. c	32. b
7. a	7. c	33. d	7. b	33. a
8. d	8. b	34. d	8. a	34. a
9. b	9. b	35. c	9. b	35. d
10. b	10. d	36. d	10. b	36. c
11. b	11. a	37. b	11. b	37. a
12. a	12. d	38. a	12. c	38. d
13. c	13. b	39. c	13. d	39. d
14. d	14. c	40. c	14. b	40. c
15. b	15. d	41. c	15. d	41. d
16. d	16. d	42. a	16. a	42. a
17. b	17. a	43. a	17. b	43. c
18. a	18. b	44. b	18. b	44. a
19. b	19. d	45. d	19. c	45. c
20. a	20. b	46. d	20. d	46. c
21. d	21. c	47. c	21. a	47. b
22. b	22. d	48. a	22. c	48. a
23. b	23. a	49. b	23. b	49. d
24. c	24. d	50. b	24. b	50. c
25. a	25. c		25. b	

PART 4
Scoring

Comprehension Prompts

■ *Unit 1*

The Middle of Nowhere:
Story Elements: Character

Responses should include observations of Ayesha's negative attitude at the beginning, and her sense of wonder and contentment at the end. Students may infer that this may be Ayesha's first trip outside a city.

The Birthday Present:
Problem and Solution

Most students will say that Luke's problem is that he does not have wrapping paper for the gift. He solves this by following his mother's suggestion to wrap it in shelf paper and decorate it with animal cutouts. Some students may conclude that Luke's problem is that he does not have any friends yet. Accept any reasonable responses.

Treasure Hunters: Cause and Effect

Lillian Rade would probably sell the necklace; Michael Miller would probably try to find the owner; the team would probably study the necklace to learn about its history.

■ *Unit 2:*

The Secret Cave:
Make Generalizations

Advice will probably include the following: leave a note telling where the hiker is going and when he or she will be back; avoid riverbeds; pay attention to warning signs of bad weather. Accept any reasonable answer.

Hands Across Time: Fact and Nonfact.

Responses should include descriptions of how the tools are made and dates of the Stone and Copper Ages. Students may also mention the length of time it takes to make the tools.

The Golden Cloak: Main Idea

"The Golden Cloak," is mainly about Singing Eagle's foolish pursuit of revenge on the sun, after the sun destroys his beautiful cloak. Eventually, Singing Eagle sees that his revenge hurts everyone, so he lets the sun go.

PART 4
Scoring

■ Unit 3:

Stan Herd, Crop Artist:
Steps in a Process

Responses may include the following steps, in order:

◆ Make a drawing on paper.

◆ Transfer the drawing to the garden patch.

◆ Cut the outlines of the drawing into the earth.

◆ Fill in the sections of the drawing with different plants.

Tracy's New Computer:
Sequence of Events

Responses may include the following, in order:

◆ She entered a contest and won a computer.

◆ She volunteered to do her English report on her new computer.

◆ She had trouble setting up the computer.

◆ She typed very slowly, and accidentally erased her work.

◆ It was so late, her mother made her go to bed without having done her report.

◆ She felt bad the next day at school because she did not have her report done.

Johnny Appleseed: Summarize

Most students will mention the following details: apple vinegar kept food from spoiling; apple cider was a popular drink; and cider could be traded at the store for necessities.

■ Unit 4

Sharks: Important
and Unimportant Information

Most facts in the article support the idea that sharks are not very dangerous to swimmers. These facts include the following: some eat only plankton and tiny fish; sharks rarely attack humans; some live only in cold water or deep water; some grow only to 3 feet long. Some students may feel that sharks are a danger to swimmers, pointing out that the great white shark is always hungry.

Birthday Sky:
Judgments and Decisions

Most students will decide that Julie's decision was not a good one because she could have hurt herself or damaged her telescope. Some may also point out that she disobeyed her mother by getting out of bed. Accept any well-reasoned response.

Mrs. Miller's Machine:
Draw Conclusions

Students may conclude that Mrs. Miller had to be intelligent, know how to use tools and build things, and know a lot about math and science.

© McGraw-Hill School Division

PART 4
Scoring

■ *Unit 5*

A Room for Two: Compare and Contrast

Damon likes to build models and goes to bed early. Brandon enjoys reading and staying up late. Some students may say that Brandon is more resourceful than Damon, because he came up with the solution to their problem.

The First Shoes: Make Inferences

Responses may include the following information: he saw that others walked without problems, sometimes the pain affected his decision-making, and people laughed when he walked by.

What to Buy Rover?: Author's Purpose, Point of View

Students should advise buying any of the products mentioned in the article except the doggie hiking boots or doggie watch.

■ *Unit 6*

Jazz Giant: Cause and Effect

Response may include these facts: Armstrong learned to play the cornet at this special school. After he left the school, he played the cornet for pay at night. Later, he learned to play the trumpet, which is like the cornet, and he eventually became famous playing the trumpet.

Breaking into Broadcasting: Sequence of Events

The letter will probably include the following events:

◆ seeing the ad in the paper

◆ calling the TV station

◆ writing a letter to the producer and continuing to call

◆ getting the interview and answering the question correctly

◆ going to mini broadcasting school

◆ taking turns being both a reporter and an anchor on the air

Devin's Decision: Draw Conclusions

Responses will vary, but should include reasons why they agree or disagree with Devin's decision to drop softball and swimming.

PART 4
Scoring

A Fun Way to Remember: Steps in a Process

Students should include the following steps, in order:

◆ Smear the track side of the mold with petroleum jelly.

◆ Place another cardboard circle over the mold.

◆ Mix another batch of plaster, then pour it over the mold.

◆ When the plaster is dry, separate the mold from the casting.

Fitting In: Story Elements: Character

Most students will point out that Vonda is sometimes impatient with her brother, such as when he squeaks; that she is kind, because she apologizes when she sees his feelings have been hurt; and that she enjoys music.

The Storage Closet: Make Inferences

Responses may include the following: Alma wanted a mouse, and there was one in the closet; she didn't want to put it in a cage; she wanted to visit the mouse in the closet; she wanted to play with the objects in the closet.

Jacqueline's Gift: Make Generalizations

Responses may describe a woman who is brave and hardworking, and a dedicated and excellent pilot.

PART 4
Scoring

■ *End-Year*

A Thrilling Ride: Judgments and Decisions

Responses will probably state that the ride was very exciting and different from anything experienced before, and may mention beautiful scenery seen along the way on the long ride.

My Business Plan: Draw Conclusions

Most students will judge that the plan will work, because the narrator has researched well before deciding on this business plan. He knows how much he can earn for each lawn, knows there are people who want his service, and understands his expenses.

Rolling Racers: Problem and Solution

Manisha's problem was that she was very weak and was unable to push her chair efficiently. She solved the problem by learning how to push efficiently and practicing.

A Baseball Legend: Make Inferences

Students may infer that Jackie Robinson was a very brave man who wanted to help establish for African-Americans the right to play in major league sports, and to overcome racial prejudice in general. They may also infer that his love of baseball was very strong.

Evaluation Form

Part 4   Scoring

Student Name _____

Assessment Context(s) _____

Reading Interests, Attitudes, Appreciation

Directions: Use this form to record and evaluate information about students' reading interests, attitudes, and appreciation. Rate the student on each criterion listed below by assigning a score of 1–4, or you may note brief comments and remarks instead of assigning scores. Scoring: 1 = Needs to Improve; 2 = Fair; 3 = Good; 4 = Excellent

Date of Observation   _____   _____

Reading Interests

Selects stories and books for personal interests   _____   _____

Develops personal reading and writing interests   _____   _____

Makes connections between personal life and literature   _____   _____

Attitudes

Chooses to read and write for a variety of purposes   _____   _____

Shares, reviews, and recommends books to others   _____   _____

Develops an awareness of the classroom as a community of learners which values cooperation, fair play, and respect for others and self   _____   _____

Appreciation

Appreciates multicultural perspectives   _____   _____

Appreciates and values diverse points of view   _____   _____

Demonstrates awareness of cultural backgrounds, experiences, emotions, and ideas of self and others through literature   _____   _____

Recognizes cultural attitudes and customs in literary selections   _____   _____

Appreciates words and the sound of language   _____   _____

Appreciates the writer's craft   _____   _____

Appreciates artistic styles, media, and techniques   _____   _____

Summary Score   _____   _____

Notes and Comments

Class Summary

Part 4   Scoring

Grade 5   Unit _____

Student Name	Comprehension	Vocabulary Strategies	Study Skills	Listening	Writing

Class Record

Directions: Record students' scores on each assessment administered during the year.

Student Name	Unit 1	Unit 2	Unit 3	Mid-Year	Unit 4	Unit 5	Unit 6	End-Year

Teacher's Notes

Introduction

This program provides a number of different theme-related materials in each level and unit, which may be used as alternative contexts for teaching strategies in different ways or offering opportunities for additional practice. This section of the manual includes two kinds of charts. You may want to use these resources to help plan reteaching activities.

◆ **Assessment Informs Instruction**

Alternative Contexts for Reteaching Skills and Strategies

These charts, organized by unit, list specific activities suitable for reteaching skills and strategies in each unit of Grade 5. They provide references for all of the following resources:

Teacher's Edition

Skills Minilessons/Prevention/Intervention

Leveled Book—Easy

Reteach Blackline Masters

Practice Book

Extend Blackline Masters

Alternate Teaching Strategy

Language Support: Lessons in Practice Blackline Masters

Unit Writing Process Lessons

Meeting Individual Needs for Writing—Easy

◆ **Content Analysis Chart**

This chart, organized by skill, lists collectively the program skills and strategies measured in the Unit Assessments, Mid-Year Assessment, and End-Year Assessment.

Grade 5 Unit 1
Alternative Contexts for Reteaching Skills and Strategies

Skills and Strategies	TEACHER'S EDITION		Leveled Books-Easy	Reteaching Blackline Masters	Practice Book	Extend Blackline Masters
	Skills Minilessons	Prevention/ Intervention				
Reading			Dan's Time; Kelley in Charge; Franklin Delano Roosevelt; Diego's Sea Adventure			
Comprehension Strategies						
Problem and Solution	49			1, 5, 20, 233	1, 5, 20, 233	1, 5, 20, 233
Make Inferences	77			6, 13, 27	6, 13, 27	6, 13, 27
Story Elements				8, 12, 22, 26	8, 12, 22, 26	8, 12, 22, 26
Cause and Effect	35			15, 19, 29	15, 19, 29	15, 19, 29
Vocabulary Strategies						
Antonyms and Synonyms						
Context Clues		53, 79, 83, 110		14, 21, 35	14, 21, 35	14, 21, 35
Study Skills						
Parts of a Book				4, 11, 18, 25, 32	4, 11, 18, 25, 32	4, 11, 18, 25, 32
Writing						
Personal Narrative						

Skills and Strategies	Alternate Teaching Strategies	Language Support	Unit Writing Process Lessons	Meeting Individual Needs for Writing
Reading				
Comprehension Strategies				
Problem and Solution	T60	7, 23, 38		
Make Inferences	T62	7, 15, 31		
Story Elements	T64	14, 30		
cause and Effect	T66	22		
Vocabulary Strategies				
Antonyms and Synonyms	T63	8, 32, 39		
Context Clues	T65	16, 24, 40		
Study Skills				
Parts of a Book	T61			
Writing				
Personal Narrative			135A–135F	43L, 65L, 93L, 123L, 133L

Grade 5 Unit 2

Alternative Contexts for Reteaching Skills and Strategies

Skills and Strategies	TEACHER'S EDITION		Leveled Books-Easy	Reteaching Blackline Masters	Practice Book	Extend Blackline Masters
	Skills Minilessons	Prevention/ Intervention				
Reading			*From Dust to Hope; Through a Mountain and Under a Sea; The Mills Green Team; Blue-Face Blues*			
Comprehension Strategies						
Make Predictions				38, 42, 49, 63	38, 42, 49, 63	38, 42, 49, 63
Form Generalizations				43, 50, 64, 70	43, 50, 64, 70	43, 50, 64, 70
Fact and Nonfact				45, 49, 57	45, 49, 57	45, 49, 57
Main Idea	183			52, 56, 66	52, 56, 66	52, 56, 66
Vocabulary Strategies						
Compound Words				44, 65, 71	44, 65, 71	44, 65, 71
Inflectional Endings				51, 58, 72	51, 58, 72	51, 58, 72
Study Skills						
Reference Sources				41, 48, 55, 62, 69	41, 48, 55, 62, 69	41, 48, 55, 62, 69
Writing						
Writing to Persuade						

Skills and Strategies	Alternate Teaching Strategies	Language Support	Unit Writing Process Lessons	Meeting Individual Needs for Writing
Reading				
Comprehension Strategies				
Make Predictions	T60	46, 70		
Form Generalizations	T62	47, 55, 71, 78		
Fact and Nonfact	T64	54, 63		
Main Idea	T66	62		
Vocabulary Strategies				
Compound Words	T63	48, 72, 79		
Inflectional Endings	T65	56, 64, 80		
Study Skills				
Reference Sources	T61			
Writing				
Writing to Persuade			253A–253F	165L, 199L, 221L, 241L, 251L

Grade 5 Unit 3

Alternative Contexts for Reteaching Skills and Strategies

Skills and Strategies	TEACHER'S EDITION		Leveled Books-Easy	Reteaching Blackline Masters	Practice Book	Extend Blackline Masters
	Skills Minilessons	Prevention/ Intervention				
Reading			Dancers in the Spotlight; Human Writes!; Dear Diary; Maya's Mural			
Comprehension Strategies						
Steps in a Process				75, 79, 89, 93	75, 79, 89, 93	75, 79, 89, 93
Summarize	261, 297, 333, 361			80, 87, 101	80, 87, 101	80, 87, 101
Sequence of Events				82, 86, 94, 103	82, 86, 94, 103	82, 86, 94, 103
Author's Purpose, Point of View				96, 100, 107	96, 100, 107	96, 100, 107
Vocabulary Strategies						
Multiple-Meaning Words		313, 348, 355		81, 102, 108	81, 102, 108	81, 102, 108
Figurative Language				88, 95, 109	88, 95, 109	88, 95, 109
Study Skills						
Various Texts				78, 85, 92, 99, 106	78, 85, 92, 99, 106	78, 85, 92, 99, 106
Writing						
Writing To Explain						

© McGraw-Hill School Division

Skills and Strategies	Alternate Teaching Strategies	Language Support	Unit Writing Process Lessons	Meeting Individual Needs for Writing
Reading				
Comprehension Strategies				
Steps in a Process	T62	82, 102		
Summarize	T64	87, 95, 111		
Sequence of Events	T66	94, 103		
Author's Purpose, Point of View	T68	110, 118		
Vocabulary Strategies				
Multiple-Meaning Words	T65	88, 112, 119		
Figurative Language	T67	96, 104, 120		
Study Skills				
Various Texts	T63			
Writing				
Writing to Explain			383A–383F	273L, 307L, 339L, 371L, 381L

Grade 5 Unit 4

Alternative Contexts for Reteaching Skills and Strategies

Skills and Strategies	TEACHER'S EDITION Skills Minilessons	Prevention/ Intervention	Leveled Books-Easy	Reteaching Blackline Masters	Practice Book	Extend Blackline Masters
Reading			*The Eye of the Hurricane; On Track; Tourist Trap Island; Tornado!*			
Comprehension Strategies						
Judgments and Decisions				112, 116, 133, 137	112, 116, 133, 137	112, 116, 133, 137
Draw Conclusions	475			117, 124, 138	117, 124, 138	117, 124, 138
Important and Unimportant Information				119, 123, 131, 144	119, 123, 131, 144	119, 123, 131, 144
Fact and Nonfact				126, 130, 140	126, 130, 140	126, 130, 140
Vocabulary Strategies						
Suffixes (-less, -ment)	393, 421, 445			118, 132, 146	118, 132, 146	118, 132, 146
Root Words	423, 443			125, 139, 145	125, 139, 145	125, 139, 145
Study Skills						
Graphic Aids				115, 122, 129, 136, 143	115, 122, 129, 136, 143	115, 122, 129, 136, 143
Writing						
Expository Writing						

Skills and Strategies		Alternate Teaching Strategies	Language Support	Unit Writing Process Lessons	Meeting Individual Needs for Writing
Reading					
Comprehension Strategies					
	Judgments and Decisions	T60	126, 150		
	Draw Conclusions	T62	127, 135, 151		
	Important and Unimportant Information	T64	134, 143, 158		
	Fact and Nonfact	T66	142		
Vocabulary Strategies					
	Suffixes (-less, -ment)	T63	128, 144, 160		
	Root Words	T65	136, 152, 159		
Study Skills					
	Graphic Aids	T61			
Writing					
	Expository Writing			503A–503F	407L, 431L, 463L, 491L, 501L

Grade 5 Unit 5
Alternative Contexts for Reteaching Skills and Strategies

Skills and Strategies	TEACHER'S EDITION		Leveled Books-Easy	Reteaching Blackline Masters	Practice Book	Extend Blackline Masters
	Skills Minilessons	Prevention/ Intervention				
Reading			*The Riddle of the Sphinx; On the Ball; Teammates; Unusual Bridges*			
Comprehension Strategies						
Compare and Contrast				153	153	153
Author's Purpose, Point of View				156, 160, 168, 181	156, 160, 168, 181	156, 160, 168, 181
Problem and Solution				163, 167, 177	163, 167, 177	163, 167, 177
Make Inferences	589			154, 161	154, 161	154, 161
Vocabulary Strategies						
Context Clues	519	511, 523, 541, 569, 587, 595		155, 169, 182	155, 169, 182	155, 169, 182
Prefixes				162, 176, 183	162, 176, 183	162, 176, 183
Study Skills						
Follow Directions				152	152	152
Read Signs				159	159	159
Read a News Article				166	166	166
Read a Help-Wanted Ad				173	173	173
Read an Editorial				180	180	180
Writing						
Writing to Compare						

Skills and Strategies	Alternate Teaching Strategies	Language Support	Unit Writing Process Lessons	Meeting Individual Needs for Writing
Reading				
Comprehension Strategies				
Compare and Contrast	T60	166, 190		
Author's Purpose, Point of View	T64	174, 183, 198		
Problem and Solution	T65	182		
Make Inferences	T62	167, 175, 191		
Vocabulary Strategies				
Context Clues	T63	168, 184, 199		
Prefixes	T65	176, 192, 200		
Study Skills				
Follow Directions	T61			
Read Signs				
Read a News Article				
Read a Help-Wanted Ad				
Read an Editorial				
Writing				
Writing to Compare			613A–613F	513L, 553L, 579L, 601;, 611L

PART 5
Reteaching

Grade 5 Unit 6

Alternative Contexts for Reteaching Skills and Strategies

Skills and Strategies	TEACHER'S EDITION		Leveled Books-Easy	Reteaching Blackline Masters	Practice Book	Extend Blackline Masters
	Skills Minilessons	Prevention/ Intervention				
Reading			*Flight of the Trumpeters; A Matter of Time; Unusual Occupations; The Day My Grandpa Voted*			
Comprehension Strategies						
Judgments and Decisions					186, 190, 207, 211	186, 190, 207, 211
Cause and Effect				193, 197, 205, 218	193, 197, 205, 218	193, 197, 205, 218
Draw Conclusions	687			191, 198, 212	191, 198, 212	191, 198, 212
Sequence of Events				200, 214, 204	200, 214, 204	200, 214, 204
Vocabulary Strategies						
Context Clues	691, 703	620, 688, 705		192, 206, 220	192, 206, 220	1192, 206, 220
Antonyms and Synonyms		679		199, 213, 219	199, 213, 219	199, 213, 219
Study Skills						
Read a Map				189	189	189
Conduct an Interview				196	196	196
Choose Reference Sources				203	203	203
Use an Outline				210	210	210
Use an Encyclopedia				217	217	217
Writing						
Write a Story						

PART 5
Reteaching

Skills and Strategies	Alternate Teaching Strategies	Language Support	Unit Writing Process Lessons	Meeting Individual Needs for Writing
Reading				
Comprehension Strategies				
Judgments and Decisions	T60	205, 206, 230		
Cause and Effect	T64	214, 223, 238		
Draw Conclusions	T62	207, 215, 231		
Sequence of Events	T66	222		
Vocabulary Strategies				
Context Clues	T63	208, 224, 240		
Antonyms and Synonyms	T65	216, 232, 239		
Study Skills				
Read a Map				
Conduct an Interview				
Choose Reference Sources	T61			
Use an Outline				
Use an Encyclopedia				
Writing				
Write a Story			729A–729F	647L, 673L, 697L, 717L, 727L

Content Analysis Chart

The chart below shows the program skills and strategies tested in the Unit Assessments (1–6), Mid-Year Assessment (M), and End-Year Assessment (E), both Comprehension Prompt and Multiple Choice forms.

	1	2	3	4	5	6	M	E
READING Comprehension								
Problem and Solution	●				●		●	●
Make Inferences	●				●		●	●
Story Elements	●						●	
Cause and Effect	●					●	●	●
Make Predictions		●					●	
Form Generalizations		●					●	
Fact and Nonfact		●		●			●	●
Main Idea		●					●	
Steps in a Process			●				●	
Summarize			●				●	
Sequence of Events			●			●	●	●
Author's Purpose, Point of View			●		●		●	●
Judgments and Decisions				●		●	●	
Draw Conclusions				●		●	●	
Important and Unimportant Information				●			●	
Compare and Contrast								●
VOCABULARY STRATEGIES Anyonyms and Synonyms	●					●	●	●
Context Clues	●				●	●	●	●
Compound Words		●					●	
Inflectional Endings		●					●	
Multiple Meaning Words			●				●	
Figurative Language			●				●	
Suffixes				●				●
Root Words				●				●
Prefixes					●			●
STUDY SKILLS Parts of a Book	●						●	
Reference Sources		●					●	
Various Texts			●		●		●	●
Graphic Aids				●				●
Use an Outline						●		●
Choose a Resource						●		●
WRITING Personal Narrative	●						●	
Writing to Persuade		●					●	
Writing to Explain			●				●	
Expository Writing				●				●
Writing to Compare					●			●
Writing a Story						●		●

Teacher's Notes

McGRAW-HILL READING

Unit Test

Student Name: _____

Date: _____

Grade 5 • Unit 1

The Middle of Nowhere

Ayesha looked out the window as the bus pulled away. She didn't even wave back at her parents. She was angry with them for sending her to camp. When they had first shown her the brochure that described Camp Lakota, she said, "What's wrong with staying home? All my friends are here."

"You'll make new friends," her parents said. "There's nothing like camping in the middle of the woods to help you appreciate nature." You mean in the middle of nowhere," sniffed Ayesha.

Nowhere was exactly where she was headed—on a hulking bus with a bunch of strangers. She stared out at the deep forests as the bus wound around the steep mountain roads. Eventually, the bus exited onto a side road that soon deteriorated into a bumpy dirt path. Finally, it pulled into a long driveway that cut through the dark forest. It stopped in a sunny clearing.

"Welcome to Camp Lakota," sang out the counselors as the campers got off the bus.

"You mean Camp in the Middle of Nowhere," Ayesha said with an angry scowl. The counselors replied with smiles.

By the time Ayesha and the others were settled into tents, it was time for dinner in the main cabin. After sitting around a crackling campfire, breathing in the rich pine air, they trooped back to the tents and got ready for bed. Then a counselor came in and told them to roll up the sides of the tent.

"Why?" asked Ayesha. "You'll see," answered the counselor.

As the girls got into their bunks, all the counselors in all the tents blew out the oil lamps at the same time. Suddenly, Ayesha was surrounded by the darkest dark she had ever known.

"Look up at the sky," said the counselor. Ayesha saw a great river of stars. "What is it?" she breathed in wonder. "The Milky Way," said the counselor. "You can only see it when you're far from city lights— in the middle of nowhere."

Ayesha grew as silent as the stars. The middle of nowhere had turned out a beautiful place to be.

Name _____ Date _____

♦ Fill in the circle next to the correct answer.

1. Ayesha's problem at the beginning of the story is that _____ .
   - ⓐ she is afraid to leave home
   - ⓑ her parents vacation is cancelled
   - ⓒ she doesn't want to go to camp
   - ⓓ she doesn't like to ride buses

2. Ayesha's problem is solved when she begins to _____ .
   - ⓐ appreciate her surroundings
   - ⓑ make friends with other campers
   - ⓒ talk to her counselors
   - ⓓ hate Camp Lakota

3. You can guess from the counselors' reaction to Ayesha's anger that they _____ .
   - ⓐ planned to trick Ayesha
   - ⓑ had never been counselors before
   - ⓒ wanted to send Ayesha home
   - ⓓ knew how to deal with unhappy campers

4. Ayesha was able to see the Milky Way because _____ .
   - ⓐ the counselors pointed it out
   - ⓑ she was far from the city lights
   - ⓒ she learned about it in school
   - ⓓ it is only visible once a year

5. A word that means the opposite of **scowl** is _____ .
   - ⓐ smile
   - ⓑ sniff
   - ⓒ answer
   - ⓓ clearing

6. Ayesha looked at a **brochure** of Camp Lakota. A **brochure** is a _____
   - ⓐ uniform
   - ⓑ campfire
   - ⓒ ticket
   - ⓓ booklet

GO ON ▶

Comprehension: 1-4 **Vocabulary Strategies:** 5, 6   Grade 5/Unit 1

The Birthday Present

Luke was grinning as he got off the bus. He almost rocketed into the car. His mother kissed him and said, "We've been here two weeks now, and every other day you've looked as gloomy as a rain cloud. Did you get an A on your test?"

"Even better," answered Luke. "I've been invited to a birthday party Saturday night. And I thought no one liked me because I'm the new kid."

"That is spectacular news," agreed his mother. "Whose party is it?"

"Kyle's," said Luke. "He wants to be an animal doctor, so I'm going downtown on Saturday to get him something about animals for a present."

On Saturday, Luke went from store to store until he found exactly the perfect present—a book about a veterinarian who worked at a zoo. He needed to find exactly the perfect wrapping paper, but first he decided to sit down and browse through the book. It had fascinating pictures of a veterinarian doing great things like bandaging a rhinoceros's leg. The next thing Luke knew, a loudspeaker was blaring out, "Closing time!"

Luke hadn't bought any wrapping paper yet! How could he wrap the present? Most of his family's possessions, including wrapping paper and tape, were still in cartons. He felt miserable when he got home. "I may as well skip the party—I can't take an unwrapped gift to Kyle," he told his mom.

"Don't fret," she said. "I've been lining shelves with this white paper. You can wrap the book in it, and you can cut out some animal pictures from this wildlife magazine for decoration."

"But what about tape?" asked Luke.

"One minute," said his mother as she disappeared into the bathroom. She returned triumphantly, waving a box of adhesive bandages.

"What are those for? I didn't cut myself?" said Luke in a puzzled voice.

"You're going to use them instead of tape," explained his mother.

Still doubtful, Luke did as she said. He even stuck on the animal pictures with adhesive bandages. Then he went off to the party. When he got home, he burst into his mother's room.

"Guess what!" he said. "It was exactly the perfect present in exactly the perfect paper. Kyle really liked it. He said it was his only present where the outside matched the inside."

♦ Fill in the circle next to the correct answer.

7. Luke's problem in the story is that he _____ .

    ⓐ needs to wrap a present   ⓑ failed a test

    ⓒ is not liked by his classmates   ⓓ forgot to buy a present

8. Luke solves his problem by _____ .

    ⓐ studying hard   ⓑ using shelf paper and adhesive bandages

    ⓒ calling his mother for a ride   ⓓ giving away one of his own books

9. You can guess that Luke's unhappiness at the beginning of school was because _____ .

    ⓐ he didn't like his teachers   ⓑ he had to walk home every day

    ⓒ he hadn't made any friends yet   ⓓ he hurt his leg

10. The events in the story suggest that Luke's mother _____ .

    ⓐ has clever ideas   ⓑ likes to move around a lot

    ⓒ used to be a nurse   ⓓ likes to drive

11. Luke's mother said that his news was **spectacular**. This means that it was _____ .

    ⓐ frightening   ⓑ unhappy

    ⓒ funny   ⓓ wonderful

12. When Luke's mother tells him not to **fret**, she is telling him not to _____ .

    ⓐ worry   ⓑ wrap the gift

    ⓒ grin   ⓓ return

GO ON ▶

Treasure Hunters

Many people get stars in their eyes at the thought of buried treasure. They imagine pirate ships and chests filled with gold. Some people do more than dream about buried treasure. They use metal detectors to hunt for it.

These machines use radio waves to locate metal objects underground. When a wave hits one, it bounces back to the machine. The device then makes noise. A good one can point out objects buried up to eight inches deep.

You can see people using metal detectors on beaches and empty lots, in fields and parks. Treasure hunters come from all walks of life. They are joined by the thrill of searching for lost riches. Some even find them. A woman named Lillian Rade recently unearthed an old silver coin in a potato field. Minted in 1652, the coin was worth more than $35,000. Digging it up was an exciting moment.

Michael Miller hunts for treasure on beaches. There he finds gold and silver jewelry lost in the sand. If he thinks he can find the original owner, he takes out a newspaper ad. Miller enjoys treasure hunting. But he also uses it to protect the environment. Often, he'll dig up only a rusty old nail or can. He doesn't leave these dangerous things on the beaches he loves. Instead, he throws them in a garbage can. It's his way of keeping the beaches safe.

Treasure hunters also help us learn about the past. One group went to Romania and found statues more than a thousand years old. Another team dug up bullets on an old battlefield to help figure out how many people had once fought there. Both trips were great adventures.

Few treasure hunters ever make a fortune. But they do prize the thank-you letters they get from grateful owners of lost objects found and returned. For most treasure hunters, the excitement of the search is reward enough. Or, as a treasure hunter might say, "You just never know what we'll dig up next!"

♦ Fill in the circle next to the correct answer.

13. Treasure hunters dug up bullets on an old battlefield because they wanted to
_____ .

　ⓐ find out how many people fought there

　ⓑ find out what kinds of guns were used

　ⓒ sell the bullets to collectors

　ⓓ melt the bullets for the silver

14. If Michael Miller found a bracelet with someone's name written on it he would
probably _____ .

　ⓐ try to sell it　　　　　　ⓑ try to find the owner

　ⓒ give it to someone else　　ⓓ keep it for himself

15. A metal detector makes noise when it finds an object because _____ .

　ⓐ the radio waves bounce back to it　ⓑ it has a special sensor

　ⓒ it is low on batteries　　　　　　ⓓ it works like a clock

16. Most people who use metal detectors do so because they _____ .

　ⓐ expect to find riches　　ⓑ enjoy the thrill of the search

　ⓒ lost something important　ⓓ want to clean the beaches

17. A woman **unearthed** an old coin. A synonym for **unearthed** is _____
.

　ⓐ come from　　ⓑ think of

　ⓒ dug up　　　　ⓓ bounced back from

18. In the story, we read: "The **device** then makes noise." The word **device** refers
to _____

　ⓐ a treasure hunter　　ⓑ the metal detector

　ⓒ a silver coin　　　　ⓓ any piece of metal

GO ON ▶

♦ Use the **dictionary** entry below to answer the following questions.

jam¹ (jam) *verb* **1.** to squeeze into a tight space
2. to injure or crush by squeezing **3.** to fill or
block by crowding **4.** to push or shove hard
5. *Music.* to compose and play jazz without
preparing in advance *noun* **1.** many things
jammed together [a traffic *jam*] **2.** *Informal.* a
difficult situation.

jam² (jam) *noun* **1.** a sweet food made by
boiling fruit with sugar
jam *v.* **jammed, jamming** **n.,** plural **jams**

♦ Fill in the circle next to the correct answer.

19. Which sentence below uses the word **jammed** in the sense of "to push or shove hard and fast"?

   ⓐ He broke his finger when he tried to open the jammed door.

   ⓑ The cars were jammed into the parking lot.

   ⓒ The musicians jammed all night.

   ⓓ The driver jammed on the brakes.

20. Which definition describes how **jam** is used in the sentence, "We were in a real **jam** when we locked ourselves out of the house."?

   ⓐ to injure or crush by squeezing

   ⓑ a sweet food made by boiling fruit with sugar

   ⓒ a difficult situation

   ⓓ to push or shove hard and fast

♦ Use the **index** below to answer the following questions.

Age, 43

Barking, 101

Doghouses, 69, 74-76 (diagram)

Feeding, 60, 65 (chart)

Fleas, 133-134

Housebreaking, 87-90

Illness, 113, 127

Puppies, 171, 174-175 (photos)

Toys, 77-78

Training, 90-100; come, 98; down, 99;
  heel, 97; sit, 96; stay, 96

♦ Fill in the circle next to the correct answer.

21. On which page would you find information about teaching your dog to come when called?

    ⓐ 171
    ⓒ 98
    ⓑ 43
    ⓓ 101

22. On which pages could you find information about how dogs like to play?

    ⓐ 77-78
    ⓒ 74-76
    ⓑ 133-134
    ⓓ 60, 65

GO ON ➡

♦ Fill in the circle next to the correct answer.

23. In the story, Scott **ambled** in. What does **ambled** mean?

ⓐ walked quickly   ⓑ walked in a leisurely way

ⓒ ran   ⓓ shuffled his feet

24. What do you think Carmen will do next?

ⓐ make a new batch of frosting   ⓑ change the light bulb

ⓒ go wash up   ⓓ go to the bake sale

25. This story is mostly about two people who _____.

ⓐ don't like each other   ⓑ can't cook

ⓒ are friends, but are very different   ⓓ like to take their time

GO ON ➡

♦ Write a story about the first birthday you can remember. Describe what your day was like and how it felt to be one year older.

_____

_____

_____

_____

_____

_____

_____

_____

_____

_____

_____

_____

_____

_____

_____

_____

_____

_____

_____

EVALUATION CHART

GRADE FIVE

UNIT 1: *Time of My Life*

Student Name _____   **Date** _____

Reading		
COMPREHENSION STRATEGIES	/ 12	%
Problem and Solution 1, 2, 7, 8		
Make Inferences 3, 10		
Story Elements 13, 14, 16		
Cause and Effect 4, 9, 15		
VOCABULARY STRATEGIES	/ 6	%
Antonyms and Synonyms 5, 11, 12, 17		
Context Clues 6, 18		
Study Skills	/ 4	%
Parts of a Book 19 - 22		
Listening Comprehension 23–25	/ 3	%
Constructing Meaning		
(Total of above three domains)		
Open-Ended Prompts/Written Response		
Writing: Personal Narrative		
4 = Excellent		
3 = Good		
2 = Fair		
1 = Poor		
0 = Blank		
UNIT PERFORMANCE ASSESSMENT		
4 = Excellent		
3 = Good		
2 = Fair		
1 = Poor		

McGraw-Hill School Division 🐂
A Division of The McGraw·Hill Companies

McGraw-Hill School Division
Two Penn Plaza
New York, New York 10121
Printed in the United States of America
ISBN 0-02-185480-7
1 2 3 4 5 6 7 8 9 XXX 04 3 02 01 00 99

ISBN 0-02-185480-7

99701

9 780021 854806

5, U. 1

McGRAW-HILL READING

Unit Test

Student Name: _____

Date: _____

Grade 5 • Unit 2

The Secret Cave

My friend Marty thinks he's a real woodsman. Last Saturday he decided to take me to his hidden cave. We set out before daybreak. I wanted to leave the standard hiker's message for my parents, telling where we were headed and when we were coming back, in case anything happened. But Marty said, "Don't be a baby."

So I strapped on my backpack and we started out. When we got to the trail head, we found a warning that told us to watch out for flash floods. But the day was dawning bright and clear, so we went ahead.

"Where is this cave, anyway?" I asked Marty for the millionth time. He had been keeping that news a secret.

"You'll see," he answered for the millionth time. We kept going. After a few hours, we left the trail. We hiked down, down, down until we reached a dried-up old riverbed.

"This hasn't had water in it for probably a thousand years," Marty said. I believed him. Then he pointed out his hideaway. It was high in the riverbank, about ten feet up.

We scrambled inside the cave and spent the next few hours pretending we were real explorers. When we came out again, the sky had turned black and we could hear thunder. A few minutes later, buckets of rain came pelting down. It kept on for at least an hour. All of a sudden we heard a terrible roar. We looked out and saw that the dried-up old riverbed had become a river once again—a wild river—and we couldn't get out.

In a little while the rain stopped. But the river kept flowing, and rising. No one knew where we were, and it was almost nightfall. As we huddled on a ledge for what felt like forever, we heard a roaring sound again. But, this time it was a helicopter, and it was on the lookout for us!

"How could they know where we were?" I asked as the helicopter dropped a rescue sling. "I didn't leave a note for my parents."

That's when Marty admitted, "Yea, but I left one for mine."

Name _____ Date _____

♦ Fill in the circle next to the correct answer.

1. When you read that the narrator doesn't leave a note for his parents, you can guess that _____ .

   ⓐ something will go wrong   ⓑ he will get back before dark

   ⓒ his parents won't mind   ⓓ he likes to sneak off

2. When the boys hear a terrible roar, you can predict that _____ .

   ⓐ a big truck is on its way   ⓑ a wild animal is about to attack

   ⓒ the rain caused a flash flood   ⓓ the door to the cave slammed shut

3. A generalization strongly supported by this story is _____ .

   ⓐ never go hiking without leaving a note behind

   ⓑ never hike near a dried-up riverbed

   ⓒ never go inside a cave during a hike

   ⓓ never hike without a backpack

4. You can guess that from now on the narrator will _____ .

   ⓐ give up hiking   ⓑ leave a note for his parents

   ⓒ stay away from Marty   ⓓ stay in the cave during a rainstorm

5. Which of the following words from the story is NOT a compound word?

   ⓐ millionth   ⓑ backpack

   ⓒ riverbed   ⓓ nightfall

6. Which word expresses action taking place in the past?

   ⓐ thinks   ⓑ explored

   ⓒ walking   ⓓ hear

Hands Across Time

Some scientists journey back into time by trying to re-create the tools of people who lived long ago. Francois Bordes, for one, has been interested in the Stone Age since boyhood. Now a teacher, he collects the stone tools that gave that age its name. He also makes them.

After much practice, Bordes can now fashion any Stone Age tool in minutes. He uses the same toolmaking methods Stone Age people used more than ten thousand years ago. With them, he turns out perfect look-alikes.

Most Stone Age tools are made of flint. This fine-grained stone breaks away in smooth flakes. To make a spearhead, Bordes rests a flat piece of flint on his knee. He chips away at the edges with an antler. With this piece of bone, he hammers out the same leaf-point shape found in thousands of Stone Age spearheads. And, yes, the point is sharp enough to cut.

Thomas Levy studies a slightly younger age—the Copper Age of 6,500 years ago. By then, people had learned how to mine metal, and to use it for tools. In the late 1970s, Levy helped dig up a Copper Age village in Israel. Twenty years later, he went back to use Copper Age methods to make an axe.

First he and his team made a fire pit. They put some copper-bearing rocks in a clay pot and set it in the fire. They got the fire to the necessary 1,981 degrees fahrenheit by blowing on it through stalks of bamboo. It took an hour, but the rock was reduced to ashes—as well as a few small beads of copper. At this point, Levy and his group realized they hadn't made much headway. It would take them weeks to make a single axe. Even so, the project was a success. It helped the scientists understand the backbreaking labor that went into making each and every Copper Age tool.

♦ Fill in the circle next to the correct answer.

7. The main idea of this story is that _____ .
  ⓐ early toolmaking methods help us learn how people once lived
  ⓑ Stone Age tools were made of flint
  ⓒ Thomas Levy is interested in the Copper Age
  ⓓ it is easy to make an axe out of copper

8. Which of the following is not a fact from this story?
  ⓐ Frances Bordes collects stone tools
  ⓑ The Copper Age was 6,500 years ago.
  ⓒ Stone Age people made tools.
  ⓓ It was backbreaking to make tools.

9. A general statement you could make about Levy is that _____ .
  ⓐ he doesn't give up easily   ⓑ he didn't like the hard work
  ⓒ he doesn't like the Stone Age time   ⓓ he needed help on his project

10. An important fact about Stone Age tools is that _____ .
  ⓐ it is easy to make copies
  ⓑ flint is the best stone to use
  ⓒ you must use a bone to make them
  ⓓ they help us understand the Stone Age

11. Which of these words from the story is NOT a compound word?
  ⓐ headway   ⓑ look-alike
  ⓒ necessary   ⓓ fine-grained

12. Which of these words from the story is used to compare two things?
  ⓐ younger   ⓑ hammer
  ⓒ copper   ⓓ teacher

GO ON ▶

The Golden Cloak

Singing Eagle was the greatest hunter of his tribe, indeed of any tribe. One day he returned from the hunt with three golden birds. These birds were not just the color of gold. No, they were actually made of the purest gold. Singing Eagle's sister Yellow Feather was amazed. The feathers from these birds seemed to shine even brighter than the sun. With them she would make Singing Eagle the grandest cloak ever seen.

And so his clever sister did. Singing Eagle was proud to own such a magnificent garment. Donning the dazzling cloak, he set out on another hunt. At midday, he stopped to rest by a waterfall. Before he lay down, he took off the golden cloak and spread it carefully on the ground. When he woke, Singing Eagle was surprised to discover he had slept through the day. But an even bigger surprise awaited him. The feathers on his golden cloak had been burned to an ashen gray. It was no longer the most beautiful of all cloaks. It was now the ugliest. And the sun had done this terrible thing.

Singing Eagle vowed to punish the sun. Frightened by his anger, his tenderhearted sister warned him that revenge could hurt more than the intended victim. Singing Eagle ignored her and set a trap for the sun. When the sun started to rise, it slid right into the lasso Singing Eagle had hidden. The sun strained to rise, but the lasso just grew tighter. Bound by the rope, the sun became weak from its efforts and soon gave up. That day, and the next and the next, the sun did not rise.

Now everything upon the earth suffered. Without the sun, the earth grew cold. People and animals shivered and plants stopped growing. When Singing Eagle saw the results of his revenge, he began to regret what he had done. He cut the lasso that held the sun prisoner. As the sun rose and warmed the earth once again, Singing Eagle understood that the golden rays of the sun are far more beautiful than any golden feathers.

♦ Fill in the circle next to the correct answer.

13. When the sun burns the cloak to an ashen gray, you can predict that Singing Eagle _____ .

   ⓐ will laugh   ⓑ will be angry

   ⓒ will not care   ⓓ will ask for another one

14. Which prediction can you make when Singing Eagle traps the sun?

   ⓐ Yellow Feather's warning about revenge will come true.

   ⓑ All the creatures on earth will be grateful to Singing Eagle.

   ⓒ Yellow Feather will make Singing Eagle a beautiful new cloak.

   ⓓ Singing Eagle will capture the moon as well.

15. You know this story is fiction because _____ .

   ⓐ the sun doesn't rise in the sky   ⓑ Singing Eagle couldn't be a hunter

   ⓒ the sun can't be trapped by a rope   ⓓ the sun doesn't warm the earth

16. A general statement you could make about Yellow Feather is that _____ .

   ⓐ she doesn't like her brother   ⓑ she is clever and wise

   ⓒ she wants revenge   ⓓ she is afraid of her brother

17. Singing Eagle's cloak was now the _____ of all.

   ⓐ uglier   ⓑ ugliest

   ⓒ ugliness   ⓓ ugly

18. Which word used to describe Yellow Feather is a compound word?

   ⓐ tenderhearted   ⓑ clever

   ⓒ frightened   ⓓ amazed

GO ON ➤

♦ Use the **dictionary** entry below to answer the following questions.

> **light¹** (līt) ***noun*** **1.** the form of energy that can
> be seen with the eye **2.** a source of light, such
> as the sun or an electric lamp **3.** a traffic light
> **4.** a way to start a fire, such as a match
> **5.** daylight **6.** helpful knowledge [to shed *light*
> on a problem] ***adjective*** **1.** not dark; bright
> **2.** having a pale color; fair ***verb*** **1.** to set on
> fire or to catch fire **2.** to cast light on or in
> [A torch would *light* the cave.] **3.** to guide with
> a light [We would *light* our way with a lantern.]
>
> **light²** (līt) ***adjective*** **1.** not heavy **2.** mild or less
> than usual [a *light* rain] **3.** not serious **4.** silly
> **5.** moving quickly [the dancer was *light* on his
> feet.]

♦ Fill in the circle next to the correct answer.

19. What part of speech is the word **light** as used in the sentence, "The doll had **light** hair and eyes"?

    ⓐ noun   ⓑ adjective

    ⓒ verb   ⓓ pronoun

20. All of the following information about light is available in the sample entry except _____ .

    ⓐ how to spell the word   ⓑ how to pronounce the word

    ⓒ the many meanings of the word   ⓓ directions for making light with
                                         electricity

GO ON ➤

♦ Use the **encyclopedia index** below to answer the following questions.

F

Food F:101 with pictures, maps, charts

Animals A:73 with pictures, charts

Cooking C:60

Farming F:17 with pictures

Food Chain F:59 with diagram

Food and Drug Administration F:115

Health H:30

Humans H:227

Nutrients N:312

Plants P:187 with pictures, charts

Vitamins V:222 with chart

♦ Fill in the circle next to the correct answer.

21. Where would you go to find information about growing crops for food?

   ⓐ Volume A, page 73   ⓑ volume F, page 17

   ⓒ Volume V, page 222   ⓓ volume C, page 60

22. On which page in volume F does the article about the food chain begin?

   ⓐ 101   ⓑ 17

   ⓒ 59   ⓓ 115

GO ON ▶

♦ Fill in the circle next to the correct answer.

23. Mouse flexed his **puny** arms. What does **puny** mean?

   ⓐ strong   ⓑ small and weak

   ⓒ mouse-like   ⓓ phoney

24. You can predict that Wolf will _____ .

   ⓐ try to catch Rabbit   ⓑ not try to catch Rabbit again

   ⓒ let the animals go   ⓓ talk Rabbit into coming inside

25. "Never trust a flatterer" mostly means that _____ .

   ⓐ you can only trust your friends   ⓑ the flatterer may want to trick you

   ⓒ you should stay home   ⓓ you can't pass in front of Wolf's place

GO ON ➡

♦ You want to start an after-school club in an area that interests you. Write a letter to your principal about the club you'd like to start. Explain why you think it would be a good club and persuade your principal to let you start it.

_____

_____

_____

_____

_____

_____

_____

_____

_____

_____

_____

_____

_____

_____

_____

_____

_____

_____

_____

_____

EVALUATION CHART

GRADE FIVE

UNIT 2: *Building Bridges*

Student Name _____ Date _____		
Reading		
Comprehension Strategies	/12	%
Make Predictions 1, 2, 4, 13, 14		
Form Generalizations 3, 9, 16		
Fact and Nonfact 8, 10, 15		
Main Idea 7		
Vocabulary Strategies	/6	%
Compound Words 5, 11, 18		
Inflectional Endings 6, 12, 17		
Study Skills	/4	%
Reference Sources 19 - 22		
Listening Comprehension 23–25	/3	%
Constructing Meaning		
(Total of above three domains)		
Open-Ended Prompts/Written Response		
Writing: Persuasive Writing		
4 = Excellent		
3 = Good		
2 = Fair		
1 = Poor		
0 = Blank		
UNIT PERFORMANCE ASSESSMENT		
4 = Excellent		
3 = Good		
2 = Fair		
1 = Poor		

McGraw-Hill School Division
A Division of The McGraw-Hill Companies

McGraw-Hill School Division
Two Penn Plaza
New York, New York 10121
Printed in the United States of America
ISBN 0-02-185481-5
1 2 3 4 5 6 7 8 9 XXX 04 3 02 01 00 99

ISBN 0-02-185481-5

99701

9 780021 854813

5, U. 2

McGRAW-HILL READING

Unit Test

Student Name: _____

Date: _____

Grade 5 • Unit 3

Stan Herd, Crop Artist

Sometimes one moment can change a person's life. That's what happened to artist Stan Herd. On a flight across Kansas one day, he looked down at a tractor slicing a furrow across a field. Like a bolt of lightning, the idea of using the earth as a drawing tool struck him, along with the idea of using plants instead of paint for color. And so he became a crop artist.

Herd's first crop drawing was a picture of the 19th century Kiowa Chief Satanta. It took Herd months to persuade a farmer to let him carve the great chief's likeness into a 160-acre wheat field. Herd started by making a small drawing on paper. Next, a team of helpers spent a week marking the field so he could make a giant-size version of the drawing. By the time they finished, the field felt as big as an ocean. It then took Herd a day to cut the outlines of Satanta's face into the earth with a tractor. To check his work, Herd had to get a bird's eye view by flying a thousand feet over the field in a plane. That's how people have to view his art as well.

Each of Herd's pictures takes up to a year to complete, which often includes time for the crops he plants to grow. For a painting of a vase of sunflowers, Herd planted clover to form the 300-foot-high vase, and sunflowers (of course!) to form the three huge sunflowers it held.

In this new and original art form nature plays an important role. Herd's paintings change color as crops sprout, bloom, and wither. Sometimes, nature likes to play tricks. One portrait made of corn dried up when a heat wave burned the land. Wind and rain have also amused themselves by blowing away seeds and drowning plants. Herd accepts those events, because he considers his crop art part of nature's cycle of life and death.

Name _____ Date _____

♦ Fill in the circle next to the correct answer.

1. Before the helpers could mark the field, Stan Herd had to _____ .

    (a) make a drawing on paper   (b) fly over the field in a plane
    (c) plant clover and wheat   (d) plow the field with a tractor

2. What eventually happens to Herd's crop art?

    (a) It goes to a museum.   (b) It withers and dies.
    (c) It is sold to an art lover.   (d) It is covered in plastic.

3. How does the author feel about Stan Herd's crop pictures?

    (a) She thinks people should pay more money for them.
    (b) She thinks they are a waste of land and crops.
    (c) She thinks they might cause planes to crash.
    (d) She thinks they are an interesting new art form.

4. When one of Stan Herd's pictures is destroyed by nature he feels
    _____ .

    (a) accepting   (b) angry
    (c) amused   (d) foolish

5. The story says that the idea for crop art struck Herd like a bolt of lightning.
    The author means that the idea _____ .

    (a) came to him during a rainstorm   (b) gave him a headache
    (c) came to him all of a sudden   (d) was hard to understand

6. The story says that Herd had to **check** his work. What does **check** mean
    here?

    (a) pay money for   (b) make marks
    (c) stop at once   (d) look at carefully

GO ON ▶

Tracy's New Computer

Tracy felt as light as air as she walked into English class. When Mr. Green reminded the class that their reports were due the next day, Tracy couldn't hold back her news another second.

"I'm going to write my report on my new computer," she announced. "Remember that contest where you had to write an essay on why you needed a computer? Well, I won."

Mr. Green congratulated Tracy and said, "Since everyone else has to use an old-fashioned pen, I expect an extra-special report from you."

"No problem," replied Tracy.

After school, Tracy invited her friends to see the new computer. They gathered around as she took it out of the box.

"Those wires look like a pile of spaghetti," said her friend Mia.

"Don't worry, I'll sort them out," said Tracy.

"We'd better go now," continued Mia. "We still have to use crummy old pens to write our reports."

Tracy decided to start her report after dinner. With a computer, it would go quickly. She got everything plugged in, but when she tried to turn the computer on nothing happened. After a half an hour of fussing, she discovered a switch she hadn't flipped.

Tracy could finally start her report. She didn't know how to type, so she bumbled along, letter by letter. After about two hours of that, she accidentally pressed a key that made everything on the screen disappear. Try as she might, she couldn't get her words back, so she started all over. An hour or so later, she accidentally pushed the same deadly key. Now it was late, so late that Tracy's mother made her go to bed.

"You'll just have to tell your teacher what happened," her mother said.

The next day, Tracy felt like a sinking ship as she headed to school. She was the only one without a report. She explained all she had gone through.

"Why didn't you just give up and use a pen while you still had time?" Mr. Green asked her.

"Because I've got a computer now," answered Tracy. "A pen would have taken too long."

Name _____ Date _____

♦ Fill in the circle next to the correct answer.

7. Which is the best summary of this story?

   ⓐ Tracy's friends are jealous of her new computer.

   ⓑ Tracy thinks she can write her report quickly but she has trouble using her new computer.

   ⓒ Mr. Green is happy when Tracy wins a computer.

   ⓓ Tracy discovers that she doesn't know how to type.

8. What would be another good title for this story?

   ⓐ Tracy Writes a Report   ⓑ How to Win a Computer

   ⓒ Tracy and Her Mother   ⓓ Mr. Green's Class

9. What was the author trying to say when she wrote this story?

   ⓐ Entering a contest is a good way to win a new computer.

   ⓑ To keep your friends, let them use your new computer.

   ⓒ Sometimes the old ways of doing things work better.

   ⓓ Teachers should give students more of time to write reports.

10. Pens are described as "old-fashioned" and "crummy". This meant that pens _____ .

   ⓐ did not write very well   ⓑ were not valued any more

   ⓒ were all broken   ⓓ were ugly and unattractive

11. Mia said, "Those wires looked like a pile of spaghetti." She meant that the wires _____ .

   ⓐ were all tangled up   ⓑ looked good enough to eat

   ⓒ were covered with sauce   ⓓ red and yellow

12. The story says that "Tracy felt like a **sinking ship** as she walked to school." What does **sinking ship** mean here?

   ⓐ hopeful   ⓑ happy

   ⓒ hopeless   ⓓ light

GO ON ➤

Johnny Appleseed

Most people don't realize that there really was a Johnny Appleseed. This genuine American hero started life as John Chapman. Born in New England in 1774, he spent some of his boyhood years as a farm hand in nearby orchards. When he grew up, he decided to wander the land planting apple trees.

The task Johnny Appleseed set for himself was important. Planting an orchard was a way for pioneers to claim a piece of land. During his lifetime, Johnny would help start thousands of orchards. He didn't have much money to buy the seeds he needed. Instead, he went to cider mills. The millers let him pick the seeds out of the mashed-up apples.

With bags full of apple seeds, Johnny began his endless travels. When he met up with people, he would give them seeds. Often he moved through areas settlers hadn't reached yet. He would pay a few dollars for a few plots of land and plant apple seeds by the thousands. Then he would move on. A few years later, he would return. By then, the land would be thick with sturdy young apple trees. These he would sell for about 6 cents apiece. He also gave trees away.

To the settlers, apples from Johnny's trees were like gold. Apple vinegar kept their food from spoiling. And apple cider was their main drink. Cider could also be traded at the general store for precious flour, sugar, and coffee.

Johnny became a well-known sight across the land. On his head he wore a leather pot that doubled as a hat and a food dish. By choice, he slept in barns and ate wild nuts and berries. People loved him for his kind heart and wonderful stories. When he died in 1845, he was sorely missed.

Today, people can get clippings from the last known tree planted by this great man himself. Discovered in the 1990s, the tree was about 150 years old and 11 feet across. Before it blew over in a storm, members of a conservation group took thousands of cuttings. These will keep the memory of Johnny Appleseed alive.

♦ Fill in the circle next to the correct answer.

13. Which of the following is the best summary of the story?

  ⓐ Johnny Appleseed got apple seeds by picking them out of the mashed-up apples.

  ⓑ Apples from Johnny Appleseed's trees helped settlers keep their food from spoiling.

  ⓒ Johnny Appleseed helped settlers by planting apple seeds throughout the land.

  ⓓ Johnny Appleseed chose to sleep in barns and eat wild nuts and berries.

14. What would be another good title for this story?

  ⓐ The Man Who Gave Us Apple Trees ⓑ How to Make Apple Vinegar

  ⓒ The Life of Early Settlers   ⓓ Johnny Appleseed's Last Tree

15. What did Johnny Appleseed do right after he bought some land?

  ⓐ He sold apple trees.   ⓑ He planted apple seeds.

  ⓒ He went on with his travels.   ⓓ He gave away apples.

16. What happened after people took cuttings from Johnny Appleseed's last tree?

  ⓐ People made cider with the apples. ⓑ People measured the tree.

  ⓒ The tree blew over in a storm.   ⓓ Johnny Appleseed died.

17. The story says that Johnny Appleseed wore a leather pot that **doubled** as a hat and a food dish. What does **doubled** mean here?

  ⓐ turned around   ⓑ grew twice as big

  ⓒ folded   ⓓ served two purposes

18. The story says that apples were like **gold** to the settlers. What does the term like **gold** mean here?

  ⓐ precious   ⓑ heavy

  ⓒ yellow   ⓓ hard

GO ON ➤

Name _____ Date _____

♦ Use the **family tree** below to answer the following questions.

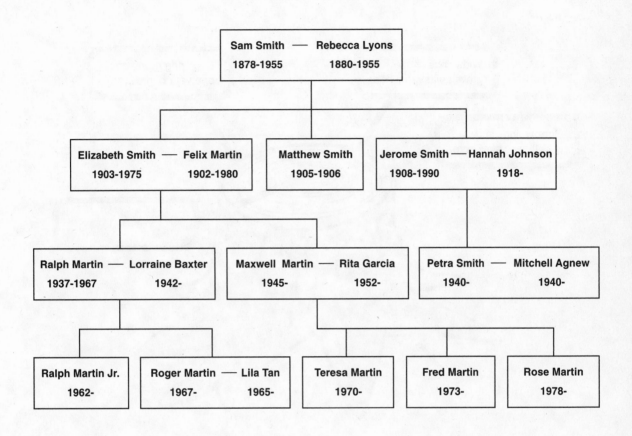

♦ Fill in the circle next to the correct answer.

19. Elizabeth Smith and Felix Martin have _____ .

   ⓐ three grandchildren   ⓑ six grandchildren

   ⓒ five grandchildren   ⓓ two grandchildren

20. Petra Smith is _____ .

   ⓐ Rose Martin's mother

   ⓑ Jerome Smith and Hannah Johnson's only child

   ⓒ Mitchell Agnew's sister

   ⓓ Ralph and Maxwell Martin's sister

♦ Use the **drawing** below to answer the following questions.

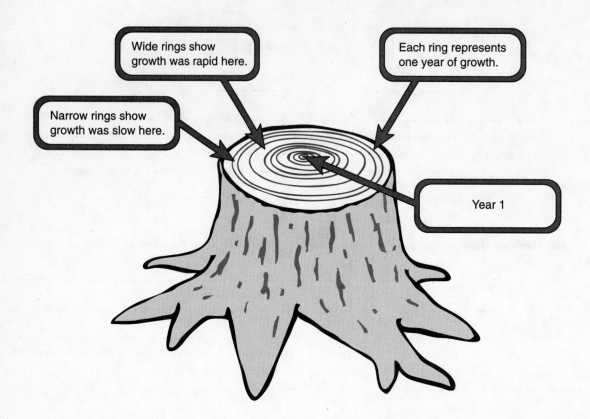

Wide rings show growth was rapid here.

Each ring represents one year of growth.

Narrow rings show growth was slow here.

Year 1

♦ Fill in the circle next to the correct answer.

21. This tree is _____ .

    ⓐ 18 years old   ⓑ 9 years old

    ⓒ 1 year old   ⓓ 4 years old

22. This tree grew the fastest _____ .

    ⓐ between years 4 and 7   ⓑ between years 7 and 9

    ⓒ between years 1 and 4   ⓓ in the third year

GO ON ➡

♦ Fill in the circle next to the correct answer.

23. His mother was an **avid** trickster. The word **avid** means _____ .

    ⓐ eager   ⓑ reluctant

    ⓒ mean   ⓓ poor

24. How do you think Jackie's mother reacted to his trick?

    ⓐ Jackie's mother didn't care one way or another.

    ⓑ Jackie's mother was terribly upset.

    ⓒ Jackie's mother was surprised but pleased.

    ⓓ Jackie's mother punished him.

25. What is this story mostly about?

    ⓐ How to make donuts out of play dough for April Fool's Day.

    ⓑ Why April Fool's Day is such an important holiday.

    ⓒ How people can get injured by tricks on April Fool's Day

    ⓓ How a boy and his mother trick each other on April Fool's Day.

GO ON ▶

♦ Write a report on how to put on a class play.

_____

_____

_____

_____

_____

_____

_____

_____

_____

_____

_____

_____

_____

_____

_____

_____

_____

_____

_____

_____

_____

EVALUATION CHART
GRADE FIVE

UNIT 3: *Imagine That*

Student Name _____   **Date** _____

Reading		
COMPREHENSION STRATEGIES	12	%
Steps in a Process 1, 2		
Summarize 7, 8, 13, 14		
Sequence of Events 15, 16		
Author's Purpose, Point of View 3, 4, 9, 10		
VOCABULARY STRATEGIES	6	%
Multiple-Meaning Words 6, 12, 17		
Figurative Language 5, 11, 18		
Study Skills	4	%
Various Texts 19 - 22		
Listening Comprehension 23–25	3	%
Constructing Meaning		
(Total of above three domains)		
Open-Ended Prompts/Written Response		
Writing: Explanatory Writing		
4 = Excellent		
3 = Good		
2 = Fair		
1 = Poor		
0 = Blank		
UNIT PERFORMANCE ASSESSMENT		
4 = Excellent		
3 = Good		
2 = Fair		
1 = Poor		

McGraw-Hill School Division 📚
A Division of The McGraw-Hill Companies

McGraw-Hill School Division
Two Penn Plaza
New York, New York 10121
Printed in the United States of America
ISBN 0-02-185482-3
1 2 3 4 5 6 7 8 9 XXX 04 3 02 01 00 99

ISBN 0-02-185482-3

99701

9 780021 854820

5, U. 3

McGRAW-HILL READING

McGRAW-HILL

Mid-Year
Test

Student Name: _____

Date: _____

Grade 5

A Fun Way to Remember

Making plaster castings of bird or animal tracks is a fun way to remember a special camping trip or other outdoor fun. And to remember times with a special friend, you can even make castings of your own handprints or footprints pressed in the sand, mud, or snow.

To make a plaster casting of an animal track, you will need an old bowl and spoon to mix the plaster, some plaster of Paris, and water. You will also need a stapler and two strips of lightweight cardboard about two inches wide. The cardboard strips need to be long enough to bend in a circle bigger than the track.

The best tracks for casting have clean edges and are not too wet. When you have found one that looks good, staple the ends of each strip together to form two circles. Set one of the circles over the track. Next, mix the plaster of Paris with water. Make sure that all the water is absorbed and the plaster is thick enough to form a peak when you pull out the spoon. Pour the plaster into the track, making sure it is completely filled. The plaster should overflow to the edges of the cardboard.

To make castings in snow, first spray the track with water. This will form an icy film over it. Then, make sure the plaster of Paris is very cold before you pour it in. This way, the plaster does not melt the snow, changing the shape of the track.

Let the plaster of Paris dry for about 20 minutes. When you pull it off the track, what you are holding in your hand is called a mold. It is backward and inside-out. To make a casting that looks just like the bird or animal track, rub the track side of the mold with petroleum jelly. Put it on the ground, track-side-up, and set the other circle of cardboard around it. Once again, you should mix up more plaster of Paris and pour it over the mold. When it is dry, you should be able to easily separate the casting and the mold.

To make your casting look more interesting, spread a thin layer of glue over it and sprinkle it with sand. You may also want to glue on a few shells, twigs, or pine cones.

♦ Fill in the circle next to the correct answer.

1. After setting the cardboard circle over the track, the next step is to
    _____ .

    ⓐ bend the cardboard into a circle   ⓑ let the plaster of Paris dry

    ⓒ separate the mold from the casting   ⓓ mix the plaster of Paris with
                                                 water

2. The author's main purpose is to explain how _____ .

    ⓐ to make a plaster casting of a track   ⓑ to make cardboard circles

    ⓒ tracks are made   ⓓ thick the plaster should be

3. The main idea of the first paragraph is _____ .

    ⓐ bird and animal tracks are beautiful

    ⓑ you can make a casting of your own handprint

    ⓒ making plaster castings is a fun way to remember a special time

    ⓓ it's easy to make castings of bird and animal tracks

4. Which of the following is a fact?

    ⓐ The cardboard should be heavy.   ⓑ You can make castings in snow.

    ⓒ You need wax to make the mold.   ⓓ The track should be very wet.

5. Before making a casting in snow, you should _____ .

    ⓐ sprinkle the track with sand   ⓑ spread a thin layer of glue over it

    ⓒ separate the casting from the mold   ⓓ spray the track with water

6. A good summary of the last paragraph is _____ .

    ⓐ You must find a pine cone.

    ⓑ Make sure the glue is thin.

    ⓒ You must glue things on your casting.

    ⓓ You can glue things to your casting to decorate it.

GO ON ▶

♦ Fill in the circle next to the correct answer.

7. The plaster should **overflow** onto the mud, sand, or snow. In this sentence, **overflow** means _____ .

   ⓐ not quite reach   ⓑ fall on the floor

   ⓒ pour over the top   ⓓ change the shape of

8. For this project, you need two strips of **lightweight** cardboard. In this sentence, **lightweight** means _____ .

   ⓐ light in color   ⓑ not heavy

   ⓒ thick   ⓓ brightly colored

9. The track should be **completely** filled with plaster. An antonym for **completely** is _____ .

   ⓐ totally   ⓑ partly

   ⓒ slowly   ⓓ quickly

10. When the plaster is mixed, all the water should be _____ by the plaster of Paris.

   ⓐ absorbing   ⓑ will absorb

   ⓒ absorb   ⓓ absorbed

GO ON ▶

Fitting In

My sister, Vonda, sings with a voice as refreshing and soft as rain. My dad's voice booms, but when he sings with Vonda, it is low and respectful, the sound of distant thunder. My voice, on the other hand, sounds a lot like the squeaky hamburger toy that the dog gnaws on. I don't exactly fit in.

Despite that, every evening after dinner, Dad makes us all sing together. "People require music," he always says. "We require it the same way we must have air to breathe." Vonda doesn't like singing with me much, and to be honest, I don't like it, either. I make everybody sound terrible.

Last night, the concert began as we cleared the table, with Vonda wincing whenever I sang too loud. When I glanced up at Dad where he stood by the dishwasher, I noticed he was singing through clenched teeth. Then, I hit a high note and Vonda's shoulders jerked like someone had stepped on her toe. She stopped singing and glared at me.

Dad said, "Vonda, don't be rude. People require music. Music is like air..."

"Well, his air squeaks!" Vonda interrupted.

I said, "I don't require music. I don't feel like singing tonight, anyway."

I must have looked hurt, because Vonda apologized and tried to convince me to sing. I didn't want to, though. Dad was not happy about it, but he said I could skip a night if that was what I wanted. I said it was.

So, they started singing again and it was excellent. Before long, I was humming along without realizing it. When I heard myself, I quit.

Vonda said, "You don't squeak when you hum, Derek."

Next, I started tapping my hand on my leg. Dad pointed at the counter, and said, "It'll sound better if you tap on the counter." It did sound better. Between songs, Dad said, "Maybe we can pick up some secondhand drums at the thrift shop, Derek. You have good rhythm."

Soon I was tapping and humming and, every once in a while, throwing in a "Whoa, whoa" or a "Uh-huh," and Vonda and I were both grinning. We sounded good.

♦ Fill in the circle next to the correct answer.

11. Which event happened first in the story?

    ⓐ The family concert began.   ⓑ Derek tapped on the counter.

    ⓒ Vonda apologized.   ⓓ Derek began to hum.

12. Where does the concert take place?

    ⓐ in the living room   ⓑ in the hallway

    ⓒ on the porch   ⓓ in the kitchen

13. After reading the story, what can you predict will happen next?

    ⓐ Vonda will not sing anymore.   ⓑ Dad will get Derek a set of drums

    ⓒ Derek will take singing lessons   ⓓ Dad will tap on the counter

14. After reading the story, what can you correctly say about Dad?

    ⓐ He is a professional drummer.   ⓑ He squeaks when he sings.

    ⓒ He enjoys music a great deal.   ⓓ He doesn't like children.

15. At the beginning of the story, Derek didn't sound good singing with his family. How was this problem solved?

    ⓐ Vonda glared at Derek.

    ⓑ Dad said it was important to have music.

    ⓒ Dad told Vonda not to be rude.

    ⓓ They decided Derek could hum and drum.

16. Which of the following is the best summary of the first paragraph?

    ⓐ Vonda has a lovely singing voice.

    ⓑ Dad and Vonda sing well together.

    ⓒ Dad makes Vonda and Derek sing every evening.

    ⓓ Dad and Vonda sing well, but Derek doesn't.

GO ON ➡

♦ Fill in the circle next to the correct answer.

17. An example of a simile, or comparison, is _____ .

ⓐ a voice as refreshing and soft as rain

ⓑ some secondhand drums

ⓒ squeak when you hum

ⓓ singing through clenched teeth

18. Vonda _____ to Derek for being rude.

ⓐ apologizing   ⓑ apologized

ⓒ apologize   ⓓ apology

19. Dad said Derek could **skip** a night. In this sentence, **skip** means _____ .

ⓐ jump over   ⓑ cause to bounce across a surface

ⓒ move by hopping   ⓓ not participate

20. An example of a metaphor is _____ .

ⓐ I don't feel like singing.

ⓑ Dad's voice is low and respectful, the sound of distant thunder.

ⓒ Dad was not thrilled about it.

ⓓ I was tapping and humming.

GO ON ▶

The Storage Closet

What Alma really wanted was a mouse. There was a perfect white one at the pet store. She imagined it curled up in her hand, scratching its nose. It only cost $1.50, but Alma was broke.

Maybe she could do chores for Mrs. Harwitz, the landlady. Alma told Mrs. Harwitz about the mouse. Mrs. Harwitz said, "How about cleaning out that storage closet under the stairs? That would be worth about five dollars." She laughed. "And if you find a mouse in there, he's yours, no charge."

Five dollars! Alma went to work, carrying newspapers out to the curb for the recycling truck to pick up, and stacking boxes of old, funny clothes in the hall. She found a chef's hat and put it on, pretending to make pizza, singing and tossing dough in the air.

There was a box that appeared to be full of rocks. When Alma looked closer, she saw that the rocks were fossils and arrowheads. One looked like a gigantic claw. A dinosaur's toenail? Alma hooked it through the air and snarled. Examining an arrowhead, she imagined a girl standing before the chief of her tribe. "Please, Father," she pleaded, "teach me to use a bow!"

On the back wall, a guitar hung by its strap from a nail. Alma took it down and strummed it gently. It made a lovely, hollow sound, reminding her of an old song. She strummed the guitar a few more times, looking for the music it seemed to hold, before picking up the dustpan and broom.

It was then that Alma saw a tiny, gray blur shoot across the floor. Mrs. Harwitz had said she might see a mouse! She imagined taking it upstairs and placing it in a plastic cage like the ones at the pet store. Suddenly that vision seemed sad. "I could visit you here," she said to the mouse. "We could have imaginary adventures together."

Alma swept, then restacked the boxes and put away the guitar and the hat. As she shut the door, Mrs. Harwitz came out, saying, "All done? I've got your five dollars, but I'm afraid the pet store may be closed."

Alma had forgotten all about the pet store. "That's okay," she said. "I've changed my mind about getting a mouse. But can I play in here sometimes?"

♦ Fill in the circle next to the correct answer.

21. Most of this story takes place in a _____ .

ⓐ farmhouse   ⓑ garage

ⓒ closet in an apartment building   ⓓ pet store

22. After Alma saw the mouse in the storage closet, she _____ .

ⓐ strummed the guitar   ⓑ found a box full of rocks

ⓒ carried newspapers out to the curb   ⓓ imagined taking the mouse upstairs

23. After reading the story, you can correctly predict that Alma will _____ .

ⓐ return to play more imaginary games in the storage closet

ⓑ ask Mrs. Harwitz if she has any more chores for her to do

ⓒ use her five dollars to buy a mouse and a plastic habitat from the pet store

ⓓ start collecting fossils and arrowheads

24. The author's main purpose in writing this story was probably _____ .

ⓐ to teach about fossils   ⓑ to tell the reader not to buy mice

ⓒ to tell how to clean a storage closet   ⓓ to entertain the reader

25. After reading this story, you could say that Mrs. Harwitz's closet _____ .

ⓐ only stored arrowheads   ⓑ stored mice

ⓒ stored many interesting things   ⓓ was always clean

26. Alma thought about a dinosaur because _____ .

ⓐ the fossils touched off her imagination

ⓑ cleaning is a boring job

ⓒ she has always been interested in dinosaurs

ⓓ she was studying dinosaurs in school

GO ON ▶

♦ Fill in the circle next to the correct answer.

27. Gently, Alma **strummed** her fingers across the guitar strings. The way it is used in this sentence, a synonym for **strummed** would be _____ .

ⓐ banged   ⓑ drummed

ⓒ brushed   ⓓ squeaked

28. Mrs. Harwitz told Alma she could have the mouse, no **charge**. In this sentence, **charge** means _____ .

ⓐ cost   ⓑ attack

ⓒ care   ⓓ blame

29. Alma carried newspapers outside to the **curb**. In this sentence, **curb** means _____ .

ⓐ bedroom   ⓑ edge of the street

ⓒ hallway   ⓓ kitchen

30. Alma pictured the mouse in a plastic **habitat** like the ones in the pet store. In this sentence, **habitat** means _____ .

ⓐ room   ⓑ burrow in the desert

ⓒ container for a pet to live in   ⓓ nest in the storeroom

GO ON ▶

Jacqueline's Gift

Jacqueline Cochran learned to fly in the early 1930s, and was a gifted female flyer in an age when most pilots were men. Time and again, she proved herself, breaking records and winning races. In 1938, she became the first woman to win the trans-American Bendix race. In 1953, she flew faster than the speed of sound, the first woman ever to do so. She set records for speed among female jet pilots more than once. The last time she did this, in 1964, she flew at a speed of 1,492.2 miles per hour.

In the 1940s, the U. S. Army needed more pilots than it could find. Jacqueline Cochran offered to train other women to fly, but the Army turned her down. For two years, she tried to convince the Army that women could fly their planes. The Army was still not ready to accept her ideas. Knowing that women could do the job, Cochran turned to the British. In England, Jacqueline Cochran helped to set up a program to train women to fly military planes. The program there was a great success.

Seeing the success of the British program convinced the U. S. Army to take Jacqueline Cochran seriously. They let her set up a training camp in West Texas and 25,000 women showed interest. Cochran wanted the program to work, so she took only the best. The women accepted into the rigorous program trained hard. Many were not able to finish it, and either dropped out or were expelled. Those who did finish learned to fly every kind of plane used by the U. S. military and showed themselves to be excellent pilots. The women who completed the program became the Women Air Force Service Pilots, or WASPs for short.

The WASPs were brave and dedicated pilots. They flew planes from factories to air bases, or from one air base to another. They also tested new airplanes and pulled flying targets for other pilots to practice with. It was hard and dangerous work and a number of them died doing it. In the end, Jacqueline Cochran was given a Distinguished Service Medal for her part in putting together the Women Air Force Service Pilots.

♦ Fill in the circle next to the correct answer.

31. When Jacqueline Cochran couldn't train women pilots for the U. S. Army, she solved the problem by _____ .

ⓐ setting records for speed   ⓑ training women in England

ⓒ training without permission   ⓓ setting up a program in Texas

32. After reading this story, you can correctly say that the WASPs _____ .

ⓐ could fly many kinds of planes   ⓑ all died while flying

ⓒ never dropped out of the program   ⓓ all got medals

33. The Army let Cochran set up a training program in the U. S. because _____ .

ⓐ she was given a Distinguished Service Medal

ⓑ Americans voted for it

ⓒ she won the trans-American Bendix race

ⓓ the training program she set up in England was a great success

34. The best title for this piece is _____ .

ⓐ The Role of Women in the Army   ⓑ Breaking Speed Records

ⓒ Flying in England   ⓓ Fearless Female Flyers

35. After reading this, you can say that Jacqueline Cochran _____ .

ⓐ could do anything   ⓑ was quite lazy

ⓒ didn't give up easily   ⓓ lived an ordinary life

36. It is a fact that _____ .

ⓐ the training program was easy to finish

ⓑ in the 1930s, most pilots were women

ⓒ Jacqueline Cochran accepted everyone who was interested in the program

ⓓ in 1938, Jacqueline Cochran was the first woman to win the Bendix race

♦ Pictured below is the **glossary** and **index** of a book. Use them to answer the questions on the following page.

Invade/Route

I

invade To go and attack in order to conquer. Enemy toops *invaded* the country.
in•vade (in vad') *verb* **invaded, invading.**

R

route A road or other course used for traveling. The *route* to the beach is steep.
route (rut *or* rout) noun, plural **routes**

Index

C

Cherokee, 8,9,21-30, 47, 55, 63
    alphabet 23, 47
    Seqouyah 23-24, 47
    Trail of Tears 55
    treaties 30,55
Cherokee, North Carolina, 30
Chickasaws, 74, 80-81
    Mississippi 74

    Shipbuilding 81
Choctaw, 75, 90-93
    Farming 91-92
    French and Indian War 90
Creek, 47,62, 70-75, 89
    Tecumseh 72-74
    treaties 47, 72, 75

♦ Fill in the circle next to the correct answer.

37. What part of speech is **invade**?

    ⓐ noun   ⓑ verb

    ⓒ adjective   ⓓ adverb

38. On what pages would you find information about the Cherokee alphabet?

    ⓐ 23, 47   ⓑ 8, 9, 21-30, 47, 55, 63

    ⓒ 75, 89   ⓓ 30, 55

39. In what order do the key words in an index appear?

    ⓐ in order of importance   ⓑ in order of use

    ⓒ in alphabetical order   ⓓ in numerical order

GO ON ▶

- In 1830 the "Indian Removal Act" was passed by the U.S. Congress. In 1838, 7,000 U.S. soldiers invaded the Cherokee Nation in Georgia. The soldiers forced men, women, and children to march almost a thousand miles to Oklahoma. About 4,000 Cherokee died along the way. The Cherokee called the route "The Trail Where They Cried." It is commonly known as the "The Trail of Tears."

- This map shows the routes the Cherokee followed. Use the **map** to answer the questions on the following page.

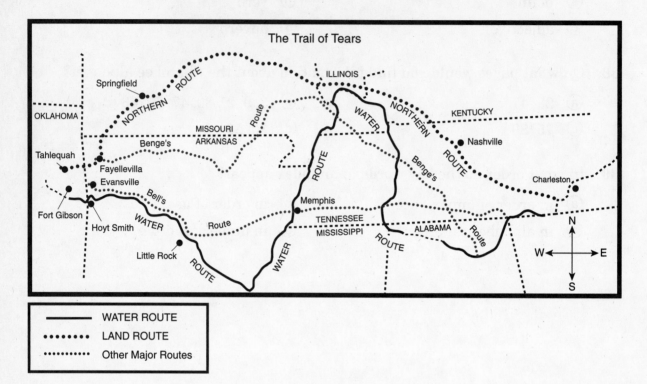

♦ Fill in the circle next to the correct answer.

40. How many different routes did the soldiers use to move the Cherokee to Oklahoma?

    ⓐ 1   ⓑ 2

    ⓒ 3   ⓓ 4

41. What was the last state they passed through before reaching Oklahoma?

    ⓐ Missouri   ⓑ Georgia

    ⓒ Arkansas   ⓓ Oklahoma

42. Which direction were the Cherokee moved?

    ⓐ east to west   ⓑ west to east

    ⓒ south to north   ⓓ east to south

GO ON ▶

♦ These drawings are a plan that a carpenter can follow to make a table. Use the **drawings** to answer the questions on the following page.

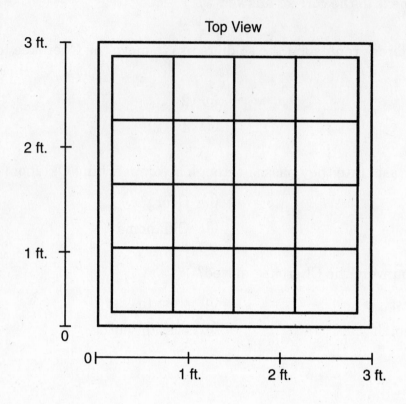

Top View

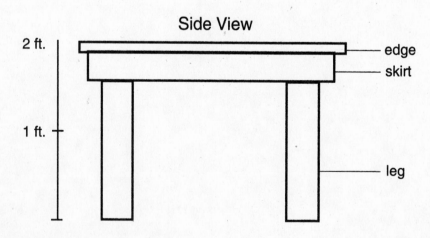

Side View

edge
skirt
leg

Name _____ Date _____

♦ Fill in the circle next to the correct answer.

43. What do the drawings show?

    ⓐ a table with a tile top   ⓑ a box of tiles on a table

    ⓒ a puzzle with a picture of a table   ⓓ a table shaped like a star

44. How tall is the table?

    ⓐ 1 foot tall   ⓑ 2 feet tall

    ⓒ 3 feet tall   ⓓ the drawings don't show that

45. How many tiles are needed to build this table?

    ⓐ four   ⓑ eight

    ⓒ twelve   ⓓ sixteen

GO ON ➤

♦ Fill in the circle next to the correct answer.

46. Jan relaxed when she saw the snake in its **terrarium**. The word **terrarium** means _____ .

  ⓐ skin
  ⓑ place on Mrs. Gates's arm
  ⓒ nest on a tree limb
  ⓓ container where it is kept

47. What did Jan do in Mrs. Gates's room during recess?

  ⓐ She played with the snake.
  ⓑ She did extra credit work.
  ⓒ She did her homework.
  ⓓ She helped polish rocks.

48. What happened after Mrs. Gates showed Jan the geode?

  ⓐ They heard voices in the hall, which meant that recess was over.
  ⓑ Mrs. Gates took the snake out of its terrarium.
  ⓒ Jan sat down to do her homework.
  ⓓ Mrs. Gates told Jan to come in and get started on her homework.

49. Which sentence tells what Jan thought about Mrs. Gates at the end of the story?

  ⓐ She was scary.
  ⓑ She was just a little different.
  ⓒ She should get rid of the snake.
  ⓓ She smiled too much.

50. Which is the best title for this story?

  ⓐ Jan Doesn't Like Snakes
  ⓑ A Little Different
  ⓒ Mrs. Gates Never Smiles
  ⓓ The Beauty of Rocks

GO ON ➤

♦ Write a story about a time when you changed your mind about a person. Tell what you thought in the beginning and why, and tell what happened to change your mind.

♦ Do you think it's okay to be "a little different?" Write an essay about it, telling why you think as you do.

♦ Think of a craft or art project you know how to do. Write an essay explaining how to do it.

_____

_____

_____

_____

_____

_____

_____

_____

_____

_____

_____

_____

_____

_____

_____

_____

_____

_____

_____

EVALUATION CHART

GRADE FIVE

MID-YEAR TEST SCORING

Student Name _____ **Date** _____

Reading		
COMPREHENSION STRATEGIES 1–6, 11–16, 21–26, 31–36	/24	%
VOCABULARY STRATEGIES 7–10, 17–20, 27–30	/12	%
Study Skills/Information Resources 37–45	/9	%
Listening Comprehension 46–50	/5	%
Open-Ended Prompts/Written Response		
Writing		
4 = Excellent		
3 = Good		
2 = Fair		
1 = Poor		
0 = Blank		

McGraw-Hill School Division
A Division of The McGraw-Hill Companies

McGraw-Hill School Division
Two Penn Plaza
New York, New York 10121
Printed in the United States of America
ISBN 0-02-185508-0
1 2 3 4 5 6 7 8 9 024 04 3 02 01 00 99

ISBN 0-02-185508-0

99701

9 780021 855087

5

Unit Test

Student Name: _____

Date: _____

Grade 5 • Unit 4

Sharks

Throughout history, people have feared sharks. Popular books tell stories of horrible shark attacks. Sharks in movies are usually terrifying. Yet scientists who study sharks have discovered many surprising things about these animals.

Many sharks have sharp-pointed teeth that they use to eat large fish and sea mammals. Others, such as the huge whale shark, feed only on plankton and tiny fish. Sharks rarely attack humans. In fact, sharks probably don't deserve their reputation as savage killers.

Sharks look and act much like their ancestors from 140 million years ago. Unlike most fish, the shark's skeleton is made up of cartilage, a tissue that is softer than bone. Also, most fish have air sacs in their bodies to help them stay afloat. Sharks do not have these air sacs. As a result, if a shark quits swimming, it sinks helplessly to the sea floor.

There are more kinds of sharks than most people imagine. Most sharks live in warm waters, but the Greenland shark lives in icy northern waters. The whale shark, which grows to 60 feet in length, is the largest fish in the world. One of the smallest sharks, the dogfish, grows only to about three feet. Some sharks live in deep waters. Others, like the sand shark, live close to shore.

A lot of attention has been focused on the great white shark. Many scientists think that it is the most dangerous shark. It has teeth that are as hard as steel. This shark is always hungry, no matter how much it eats. Like many other sharks, the great white never gets sick. It is one of the few animals that never gets cancer. It also can survive brain damage more successfully than any other animal in the world.

The study of sharks is often surprising, even to scientists. There is much more to learn about sharks. If you are interested, look for books about sharks in your library.

♦ Fill in the circle next to the correct answer.

1. All of these are facts from the selection except _____ .
   ⓐ the study of sharks is often surprising, even to scientists
   ⓑ the whale shark eats only plankton and very small fish
   ⓒ sharks are different from other fish
   ⓓ the dogfish grows only to about three feet

2. An important fact from this selection is _____ .
   ⓐ sharks are savage killers
   ⓑ if a shark quits swimming, it sinks
   ⓒ all people fear sharks
   ⓓ sharks do not like cold water

3. After reading the passage, you can conclude that _____ .
   ⓐ sharks are meat-eating fish
   ⓑ many fish live without air sacs
   ⓒ large sharks are not good hunters
   ⓓ fish like to float

4. Based on details from the passage, what can you conclude about great white sharks?
   ⓐ Scientists have gathered a lot of information about them.
   ⓑ They are about as large as the whale shark.
   ⓒ Their teeth make them more dangerous than other sharks.
   ⓓ Books and movies about these sharks are always popular.

5. **Popular** books tell stories of horrible shark attacks. The _____ of these stories are worldwide.
   ⓐ popularity
   ⓑ populous
   ⓒ popularness
   ⓓ popularally

6. The whale shark is the **largest** shark, but the dogfish is the _____ .
   ⓐ smallest
   ⓑ bravest
   ⓒ hungriest
   ⓓ quickest

GO ON ▶

Birthday Sky

Julie was too excited to sleep. Earlier that night, she had gotten a new telescope for her birthday. When the party finally ended, Julie's mom said it was too late to try out the telescope.

"We'll put your telescope together in the morning," she said. "Then you can use it tomorrow night."

Julie gazed out her window at the sparkling stars in the night sky. She thought she could see Mars twinkling red among them.

"I just can't wait!" she thought. Julie slipped out of bed and walked quietly down the stairs. The house was dark and still.

Julie opened her gift in the kitchen. Along with the telescope, she found lenses, a sighting scope, and a stand. A little package held the screws and bolts she would need to put everything together.

After about an hour, Julie thought she had everything where it belonged. She put the telescope and stand under her arm. Then she opened the back door and started down the steps. In the dark, Julie did not see Fluffy the cat. She stepped on Fluffy's tail, and the cat let out a screeching howl. Julie jumped in surprise and tripped forward. The telescope flew from her hands and landed with a thump on the ground.

Lights came on in the house. Julie's mom came to the back door and looked out. "What is going on out there?" she asked.

"It's me, Mom," Julie cried. "I couldn't wait to use my telescope. Now I've probably broken it, and I've hurt my knee too.

Julie's mom picked up the telescope and helped Julie into the house. After a quick inspection, she found no serious damage to Julie or to the telescope.

"I'm so sorry," said Julie. She was sure her mother was furious with her.

But her mother just sighed. "Okay, night owl," said her mom. "Into bed. Tomorrow evening, you can show us the craters on the moon." She paused. "And the colorful bruise you'll have on your knee."

♦ Fill in the circle next to the correct answer.

7. After the party, Julie's mom decided that _____.

   ⓐ it was too late for Julie to use her telescope

   ⓑ the telescope was too hard to put together

   ⓒ the weather was not right for looking at stars

   ⓓ they should clean up first and then look at the stars

8. Julie went outside in the dark. Why did she decide to leave the light off?

   ⓐ She could see the stars better in the dark.

   ⓑ She did not want the neighbors to see her.

   ⓒ She was in such a hurry that she forgot.

   ⓓ She did not want to wake up Fluffy.

9. If you described the telescope in the story to a friend, which of the following statements should you leave out?

   ⓐ There was a stand.   ⓑ It came with more than one lens.

   ⓒ It had a sighting scope.   ⓓ Julie put it together in the kitchen.

10. To understand why Julie fell, it is important to know that _____.

   ⓐ she opened the back door   ⓑ she stepped on Fluffy's tail

   ⓒ the telescope was under her arm   ⓓ Fluffy was Julie's cat

11. Julie was very **sorry**, in fact she was the _____ she had ever been.

   ⓐ sorriest   ⓑ sorrowful

   ⓒ sorrier   ⓓ sorriless

12. She had gotten a new **telescope**. A word using the same root word as in **telescope** is _____.

   ⓐ scope   ⓑ television

   ⓒ phone   ⓓ microphone

GO ON ➤

Mrs. Miller's Machine

Strange lights were flashing! Weird noises echoed in the night. And all of this was coming from Mrs. Miller's garage. Jana just had to see what was going on! She slipped quietly through the door.

There, in the middle of the garage, was a strange-looking machine. Mrs. Miller, a gray-haired woman in her fifties, was sitting inside it and turning dials. She didn't notice Jana.

Jana crept carefully forward. As she neared the machine, Jana tripped and fell. She landed inside, next to Mrs. Miller. Reaching out to catch herself, Jana accidentally pressed a large, red button.

"Oh, no! Look what you've done!" cried Mrs. Miller. In just a fraction of a second, the door slammed shut. The machine shook and there was a high whirring sound that hurt Jana's ears.

"Wha- What's happening?" asked Jana. "What is this machine?"

"It's a time machine. I've been secretly working on it for years," replied Mrs. Miller. "There is still much work left to do. But now you've pressed the SEND button. There's no telling where we'll find ourselves!" Mrs. Miller looked worried.

Jana was frightened and mad at herself. If only she hadn't been so careless! Suddenly, the shaking and noise stopped. Jana looked questioningly at Mrs. Miller.

"Well, let's see where we are," Mrs. Miller said bravely. She opened the machine's door. The two stepped out into what looked like Mrs. Miller's garage. They both sighed in relief.

Jana was just about to head home when the garage door opened. Coming up the driveway was the strangest thing she'd ever seen. It was kind of like a car, but it was floating on air. Other vehicles like it were moving up and down the street. The sky was filled with spacecraft buzzing around like bees.

Mrs. Miller and Jana looked at one another. This was definitely going to be an adventure.

♦ Fill in the circle next to the correct answer.

13. An important thing to know about Mrs. Miller is that she _____ .

    ⓐ has a garage with windows   ⓑ has a time machine

    ⓒ is in her fifties   ⓓ has gray hair

14. Two details that are most important in creating the action of the plot are _____ .

    ⓐ lights were flashing in Mrs. Miller's garage

    ⓑ weird noises were coming from Mrs. Miller's garage

    ⓒ Jana fell into the time machine and talked to Mrs. Miller

    ⓓ Mrs. Miller created a time machine and Jana pressed the SEND button

15. When Mrs. Miller and Jana stepped out of the machine, they were relieved because _____ .

    ⓐ the shaking stopped   ⓑ they thought it did not work

    ⓒ the noise stopped   ⓓ they had work to do in the garage

16. Based on the ending, the reader can guess that Jana and Mrs. Miller have _____ .

    ⓐ traveled into the future   ⓑ found everything just the same

    ⓒ traveled into the past   ⓓ become good friends

17. Jana had not taken **care** to watch where she was going. She was sorry she'd been so _____ .

    ⓐ careful   ⓑ careless

    ⓒ carement   ⓓ carely

18. The root word **aqua** as in **aquarium** means _____ .

    ⓐ water   ⓑ sea life

    ⓒ sea plants   ⓓ blue

GO ON ▶

Name _____ Date _____

♦ Use the **map** to answer the next two questions.

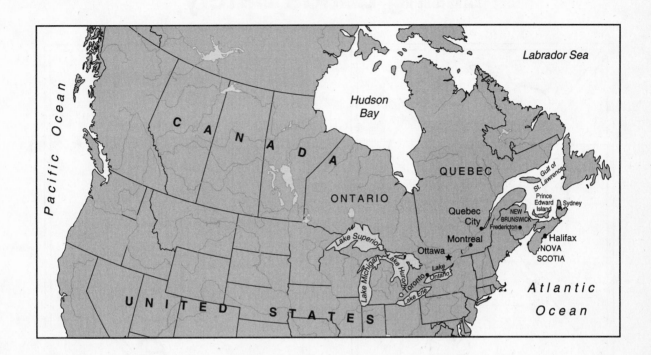

♦ Fill in the circle next to the correct answer.

19. The four lakes on the southern border of Ontario are Lake Superior, Lake Huron, Lake Erie, and _____ .

   ⓐ Lake Toronto   ⓑ Lake Ottawa

   ⓒ Lake Ontario   ⓓ Lake Montreal

20. Prince Edward Island is located in _____ .

   ⓐ Quebec   ⓑ the Gulf of St. Lawrence

   ⓒ Hudson's Bay   ⓓ the Labrador Sea

GO ON ▶

Name _____ Date _____

♦ Use the **diagram** to answer the next two questions.

Lifting Loads Safely

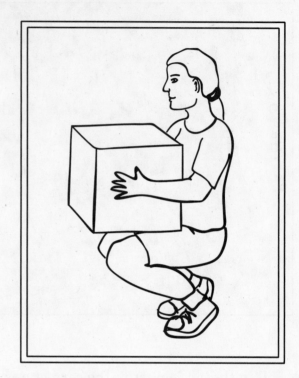

♦ Fill in the circle next to the correct answer.

21. When you lift something, it is important to _____ .

    ⓐ bend your back

    ⓑ bend your knees

    ⓒ keep the load away from your body

    ⓓ lift as quickly as possible

22. The purpose of the diagram is to show _____ .

    ⓐ how to lift loads without hurting yourself

    ⓑ that it takes two people to lift a box

    ⓒ how to exercise using a box

    ⓓ that it is not possible to lift a box without bending your back

GO ON ➡

♦ Fill in the circle next to the correct answer.

23. From this passage you can say the writer _____ .

ⓐ is afraid of insects   ⓑ is fascinated with insects

ⓒ does not know a lot about insects   ⓓ enjoys the summer

24. What conclusion can you draw about insects from this passage?

ⓐ All of the insects mentioned are helpful to people.

ⓑ Some insects are helpful to people and others are pests.

ⓒ Flying insects do harm to vegetable plants and flowers.

ⓓ Only a few insects make buzzing noises.

25. The narrator used a **magnifying** glass. A **magnifying** glass is a tool for

_____ .

ⓐ catching insects   ⓑ digging in the garden

ⓒ looking at things that are small   ⓓ measuring flowers and vegetables

GO ON ▶

♦ Write a report on surprising facts about sharks to present to your class. Use the story "Sharks" to help you write your report.

_____

_____

_____

_____

_____

_____

_____

_____

_____

_____

_____

_____

_____

_____

_____

_____

_____

_____

EVALUATION CHART

GRADE FIVE

UNIT 4: *Investigate*

Student Name _____	Date _____		
Reading			
COMPREHENSION STRATEGIES		12	%
Judgments and Decisions 7, 8			
Draw Conclusions 3, 4, 15, 16			
Important and Unimportant Information 9, 10, 13, 14			
Fact and Nonfact 1, 2			
VOCABULARY STRATEGIES		6	%
Suffixes 6, 11, 17			
Root Words 5, 12, 18			
Study Skills		4	%
Graphic Aids 19 - 22			
Listening Comprehension 23–25		3	%
Constructing Meaning			
(Total of above three domains)			
Open-Ended Prompts/Written Response			
Writing: Expository Writing			
4 = Excellent			
3 = Good			
2 = Fair			
1 = Poor			
0 = Blank			
UNIT PERFORMANCE ASSESSMENT			
4 = Excellent			
3 = Good			
2 = Fair			
1 = Poor			

McGraw-Hill School Division &
A Division of The *McGraw-Hill* Companies

McGraw-Hill School Division
Two Penn Plaza
New York, New York 10121
Printed in the United States of America
ISBN 0-02-185483-1
1 2 3 4 5 6 7 8 9 XXX 04 3 02 01 00 99

ISBN 0-02-185483-1

99701

9 780021 854837

5. U. 4

McGRAW-HILL READING

Unit Test

Student Name: _____

Date: _____

Grade 5 • Unit 5

Room for Two

"Dad, I don't understand why I can't have a room to myself," Brandon said. "Damon is really driving me nuts. His models are all over the place and I don't have anywhere to put my books. And he's always telling me to turn off the light when I still want to read. I'm sick of him intruding on my side of the room."

"I'm sorry, son. There's just no extra room in this house. We can't put your bed in Mom's home office. You'd be too much of a distraction. She needs quiet when she writes. See what else you can think of. You always have great ideas."

Brandon was really upset. As the older brother, he felt that he should have some space to himself. He decided to go for a walk and think.

The next day, Brandon asked his Dad to take him to the hardware store. They bought two low book shelves, some tacks, and two small lamps. Then they bought a colorful swatch of cloth.

That afternoon, Brandon told Damon of his plan to reorganize their living space. "Will you help me?" he asked.

"You bet I'll help. Maybe now I'll be able to get some sleep."

The boys worked all afternoon. First, they pushed each bed against a wall and put lamps next to them. Then they set up the book shelves between the beds. The book shelves divided the room into two equal parts. Next, they tacked the cloth to the ceiling right above the book shelves. Together, the shelves and the cloth formed a wall down the center of the room.

Damon put his models on one book shelf, and Brandon put his books on the other. Then they invited their parents to take a look.

"See. I have a place for my models," Damon said.

"And I can keep my lamp on as long as I want," said Brandon. "I also have a place for my books."

"Just like I said," Dad said. "You have great ideas."

Name _____ Date _____

♦ Fill in the circle next to the correct answer.

1. Brandon was unhappy because he didn't want to _____ .

   ⓐ share a room with Damon　　ⓑ put shelves in the center of the room

   ⓒ make his mother move out　　ⓓ let Damon see his books

2. Brandon solved his problem by _____ .

   ⓐ moving into his mom's office　　ⓑ selling some of his books

   ⓒ dividing the room with shelves　　ⓓ complaining to his mother

3. Brandon's idea helped Damon by giving him _____ .

   ⓐ a place to put his books　　ⓑ a place to read at night

   ⓒ a place to put his models　　ⓓ a new bedroom of his own

4. You can guess that Mom is probably a _____ .

   ⓐ clerk　　ⓑ writer

   ⓒ doctor　　ⓓ teacher

5. Damon was always going over to Brandon's side of the room. Brandon was tired of Damon's _____ .

   ⓐ detruding　　ⓑ intruding

   ⓒ retruding　　ⓓ untruding

6. When Brandon wanted to make a change in his room, he wanted to _____ it.

   ⓐ reorganize　　ⓑ disorganize

   ⓒ unorganize　　ⓓ inorganize

GO ON ▶

The First Shoes

A story told by the Plains Indians

"Ouch, ouch!" Great Chief shouted in pain with each step. He looked around the village and saw that everyone else walked with no problem. He felt ashamed to be the only one with tender feet.

Great Chief's tender feet were a problem for the whole village. Sometimes they hurt so much that the chief did not make sound decisions. Other times people turned their backs and laughed when he walked by.

One day, the Great Chief called his medicine man to his side. "You are very wise," he said. "What are you going to do to help me?"

The medicine man thought for a minute and said, "Wait two days." Then he left.

During the next two days the weavers in the village worked very hard to make a long, narrow mat of reeds. When they finished, four strong young braves unrolled the mat in front of the chief wherever he walked.

One day the braves unrolled the mat in a place where arrowheads had been cut. Sharp pieces of rock were scattered across the ground. When the sharp rocks cut through the mats and into the chief's feet, he whooped and screamed.

"You must solve this problem," he roared at the medicine man. "I will give you until the next full moon."

The medicine man went to his lodge and stared into the fire. While he thought, he noticed the hide of an elk stretched on poles. Two women were busy scraping the hair off the hide.

The next day the medicine man walked to the Chief's lodge carrying a small deerskin package under his arm. Great Chief was standing outside his lodge. The medicine man opened his bundle and took out two objects. He slipped one onto each of the chief's feet.

Great Chief slowly walked back and forth in front of the medicine man, looking at his feet. Then he picked up his bow and walked proudly away from the village wearing his new moccasins.

♦ Fill in the circle next to the correct answer.

7. The weavers in the village made a long mat of reeds because _____ .

ⓐ the medicine man told them to

ⓑ Great Chief told them to

ⓒ they needed to use extra reeds they had on hand

ⓓ they thought that it would help Great Chief's problem

8. The medicine man finally got the idea to make shoes when he _____ .

ⓐ saw the hide of an elk   ⓑ looked at Great Chief's feet

ⓒ stared at the fire   ⓓ went hunting with Great Chief

9. Great Chief asked the medicine man to help him find a way to _____ .

ⓐ clean up all the sharp rocks   ⓑ protect his tender feet

ⓒ help him make good decisions   ⓓ stretch out an elk hide on poles

10. Great Chief's tender feet were a problem for the whole village because the pain caused him to _____ .

ⓐ feel ashamed   ⓑ call off the hunts

ⓒ trip over pebbles   ⓓ make poor decisions

11. The chief proudly wore his new **moccasins**. The **moccasins** were

_____ .

ⓐ mats made of reeds   ⓑ shoes made of deerskin

ⓒ necklaces made of stones   ⓓ vests covered with arrowheads

12. The **braves** walked before the Great Chief. The **braves** were _____ .

ⓐ men of the tribe   ⓑ old weavers

ⓒ native animals   ⓓ young children

What To Buy Rover?

If you've been in a pet store, you've seen the variety of products made for dogs. Some of these products are very useful. For example, dog collars hold tags that provide an owner's phone number and address should Rover wander off. Some collars even have a red light that flashes in the dark to help dog owners locate their lost pooch.

Owners can also buy "doggy doors" for their pets. These special doors allow Rover to enter and leave a house. When the owners are home, they don't have to get off the couch to let Rover out. When they're gone, they don't have to worry that Rover needs to go outside.

The invisible fence is useful for dogs that live outdoors. The fence is placed under the ground all around a yard. When Rover walks near it, he feels a slight shock. Most dogs react by staying away from the perimeter of the yard.

Other products are helpful for dogs that live mostly indoors. Comfortable doggie beds help keep Rover off the furniture. Special gates keep him out of certain rooms, and special shampoos make him clean and free of fleas.

Unfortunately, dog owners sometimes spend their money foolishly. For example, they may buy a pair of doggie hiking boots. These "boots" are similar to socks that fit over Rover's feet. Perhaps the least useful pet product is a special watch. You may have heard that one year in a dog's life equals seven years in the life of a human. The time on the watch goes by seven times as fast as the time on a regular watch. Its inventor thought that dog owners would like to know how Rover experiences time. If you want to see time fly, this is the thing to buy. But if you want to buy something useful for Rover, you can always get a dog collar.

♦ Fill in the circle next to the correct answer.

13. According to the selection, the special watches and hiking boots for dogs are both _____ .

    ⓐ useless products   ⓑ good for all dogs

    ⓒ found in all pet stores   ⓓ helpful in finding lost dogs

14. The following would be most useful for a dog owner whose dog lives outdoors all the time.

    ⓐ an invisible fence   ⓑ a doggie door

    ⓒ a special watch   ⓓ a bed for dogs

15. The author most likely wrote this article to _____ .

    ⓐ tell stories about dogs and dog owners

    ⓑ describe products for dog owners

    ⓒ explain that some products for dogs are not useful

    ⓓ sell products to owners of dogs

16. The author would most likely agree with which statement?

    ⓐ All products for dogs cost too much money and aren't necessary.

    ⓑ Dog collars with a flashing light can be harmful to dogs.

    ⓒ Some products for dogs are useful, but some are a waste of money.

    ⓓ Almost all products for dogs make the life of a dog owner easier.

17. Dogs avoid going near the **perimeter** of the yard. The **perimeter** is the _____ .

    ⓐ outer edge of the yard   ⓑ darkest part of the yard

    ⓒ covered part of the yard   ⓓ overgrown part of the yard

18. People have created unusual products for dogs. We call these people _____ .

    ⓐ reporters   ⓑ owners

    ⓒ inventors   ⓓ visitors

♦ Use the **news article** to answer the next two questions.

Morning Edition

The Lakeside Tribune

Boy, 11, Finds Lost Necklace

By Ellen Joseph

American Lake, Feb. 4, 1999
Roger Grunwald, an 11-year old at Lakeside Elementary, made his grandmother very happy yesterday afternoon. More than 25 years ago, Roger's grandmother, Ruth Elias, lost a diamond necklace. The necklace had been in her husband's family for nearly 200 years. She remembers the day she told her husband's mother of losing the necklace. "She pretended that it did not matter because she was such a kind person. But I could see the sadness in her eyes. That made me sad too."

Ruth's sadness turned to happiness yesterday in a most unexpected way.

Roger was helping out his grandmother by replacing some floorboards in the kitchen. He carefully pulled away several old and rotting boards. The last board of the day was located near the basement door. When he pulled it loose, he was surprised to see the beautiful necklace stuck between the wall and the board.

His grandmother said, "although I am glad to have found this wonderful necklace, I am much more glad to have a wonderful grandson like Roger." Good work, Roger!

♦ Fill in the circle next to the correct answer.

19. The main idea of this article is how _____ .

    ⓐ important it is to be careful with jewelry

    ⓑ grandparents need their grandchildren to help them

    ⓒ a young boy found a necklace that his grandmother lost

    ⓓ to fix a kitchen floor

20. When did Roger find his grandmother's necklace?

    ⓐ the day before this article was written

    ⓑ over 200 years ago

    ⓒ 25 years ago

    ⓓ the day this article was written

GO ON ➡

♦ Use the editorial to answer the next two questions.

The Valley News   Morning Edition

EDITORIAL

Cats: Friends or Foes?

For many, cats make excellent, easy to care for pets. They almost take care of themselves! A cat that lives outside will learn to catch its own food. Cats are related to lions, after all. Who could ask for a better friend?

Well, Bird Watchers of the Valley could. Bird Watchers of the Valley is a group that watches and takes care of birds. Each year, cats who are outside looking for dinner, hunt for songbirds. As a result, the songbird population is getting smaller.

If you are the friend of a cat, you can be a friend to the birds, too, by keeping your cat indoors!

♦ Fill in the circle next to the correct answer.

21. The subject of this editorial is _____ .

    ⓐ how friendly cats are

    ⓑ how cats help bird watchers find birds

    ⓒ how cats kill song birds

    ⓓ how much bird watchers enjoy watching song birds

22. The author of this editorial wants cat owners to _____ .

    ⓐ keep their cats indoors   ⓑ take better care of their cats

    ⓒ teach their cats to catch birds   ⓓ get rid of their cats

GO ON ▶

♦ Fill in the circle next to the correct answer.

23. The water was **shallow**. This means that it was _____ .

   ⓐ deep   ⓑ not very deep

   ⓒ very cold   ⓓ polluted

24. What do you think Amanda will do from now on?

   ⓐ She will stay on the beach.

   ⓑ She will go in the water with flippers.

   ⓒ She will go in to swim, but wear her shoes.

   ⓓ She will take swimming lessons.

25. This story is mainly about _____ .

   ⓐ girl who is afraid of everything

   ⓑ a girl whose imagination runs away with her

   ⓒ a girl who found a way to overcome her fears

   ⓓ a girl who gets teased for wearing shoes in the water

GO ON ▶

♦ Write a report comparing a subject you enjoy studying in school with one you don't like that much. Compare and contrast the two subjects and explain what makes one more interesting than the other.

_____

_____

_____

_____

_____

_____

_____

_____

_____

_____

_____

_____

_____

_____

_____

_____

_____

_____

EVALUATION CHART

GRADE FIVE

UNIT 5: *Bright Ideas*

Student Name _____	**Date** _____	
Reading		
COMPREHENSION STRATEGIES	/ 12	%
Compare and Contrast 13, 14		
Make Inferences 3, 4, 7, 8, 15		
Author's Purpose, Point of View 16		
Problem and Solution 1, 2, 9, 10		
VOCABULARY STRATEGIES	/ 6	%
Context Clues 11, 12		
Prefixes 5, 6, 17, 18		
Study Skills	/ 4	%
Various Texts 19 - 22		
Listening Comprehension 23–25	/ 3	%
Constructing Meaning		
(Total of above three domains)		
Open-Ended Prompts/Written Response		
Writing: Writing to Compare		
4 = Excellent		
3 = Good		
2 = Fair		
1 = Poor		
0 = Blank		
UNIT PERFORMANCE ASSESSMENT		
4 = Excellent		
3 = Good		
2 = Fair		
1 = Poor		

McGraw-Hill School Division
A Division of The McGraw-Hill Companies

McGraw-Hill School Division
Two Penn Plaza
New York, New York 10121
Printed in the United States of America
ISBN 0-02-185484-X
1 2 3 4 5 6 7 8 9 024 04 3 02 01 00 99

ISBN 0-02-185484-X

99701

9 780021 854844

5, U. 5

McGRAW-HILL READING

Unit
Test

Student Name: _____

Date: _____

Grade 5 • Unit 6

Jazz Giant

"I would rather do without food than without music." These are the words Louis Armstrong used to describe his feelings about music. As a musician he was able to share this love of music with many people.

Armstrong was born in 1901, in New Orleans. He lived in a house that had no plumbing or electricity.

Music was always in the air in New Orleans. As a boy, Louis heard the lively bands that played in parades. Sometimes small groups of musicians played in the parks of the city. Louis tried to listen to music as much as he could.

Around the age of 11, Armstrong had to look for work so he could help his mother buy food. He sold newspapers and delivered coal from a mule-drawn wagon.

When Louis was about thirteen, he got into serious trouble. He was arrested and sent to a special school for boys. He joined the school marching band and played the cornet, a trumpet-like instrument.

Later, Armstrong returned to his mother's home. He hauled coal by day. At night, he played his cornet for pay. Then, in 1922, Armstrong was invited by a friend to join a band in Chicago. The friend, jazz trumpeter Joe "King" Oliver, was like a father to Louis. He gave Armstrong trumpet lessons. He also offered helpful advice.

In Chicago, Louis's career took off. He began playing the trumpet. He made recordings. Armstrong played in famous bands in Chicago and New York. He toured Europe and appeared on Broadway and in movies. He won the hearts of people around the world with his charm and his lively musical style.

Louis Armstrong became one of the most famous and well-loved musicians in the world. When he died in 1971, twenty-five thousand people paid their respects to the great giant of jazz.

♦ Fill in the circle next to the correct answer.

1. After Armstrong began selling newspapers and hauling coal, he _____ .

   ⓐ joined a jazz band   ⓑ joined the school band

   ⓒ went to reform school   ⓓ quit school

2. Which of these events happened after Louis met Joe "King" Oliver?

   ⓐ He learned to play the trumpet.   ⓑ He was paid to play his cornet.

   ⓒ He got into serious trouble.   ⓓ He went to a special school for boys.

3. Armstrong was sent to a special school for boys because he _____ .

   ⓐ got into serious trouble   ⓑ dropped out of school

   ⓒ ran away from home   ⓓ got into street fights

4. Armstrong went to Chicago because _____ .

   ⓐ he wanted to hear music there

   ⓑ a friend invited him to join a band

   ⓒ he was tired of living in New Orleans

   ⓓ he wanted to visit his father

5. Louis Armstrong earned money playing his **cornet**. A **cornet** is a kind of _____ .

   ⓐ drum   ⓑ horn

   ⓒ piano   ⓓ guitar

6. When Louis Armstrong became famous, he **toured** Europe. When he **toured** Europe, he _____ .

   ⓐ read about it   ⓑ went to live there

   ⓒ traveled and performed there   ⓓ opened a music school there

GO ON ▶

Breaking into Broadcasting

Claire has always loved sports. She enjoys playing sports. She likes watching sports events live and on television. She has often imagined herself on camera, reporting sports news, giving scores, and interviewing athletes.

One morning an ad in the newspaper caught Claire's eye. It said that a cable TV station in her town was starting a live, weekly sports program for kids. They needed kids to broadcast sports news and to interview athletes. Claire wrote down the name of the show's producer.

"I'm going to be a sportscaster," Claire announced to her friends. Some of her friends thought that was a great idea. Others said things like "A GIRL sportscaster! Who's going to watch a GIRL giving sports scores?"

Claire called the TV station. She wanted to talk to the producer. "Get in line," said a woman at the station. "A hundred other kids have called about being on the show."

Claire wasn't discouraged. She wrote a letter to the producer. She kept calling. Finally, she got an interview. The producer was surprised at how much Claire knew about sports. As a small test, he asked her, "Who's Darren Bragg?"

"Red Sox outfielder," said Claire.

She got the job.

In a mini broadcast school, Claire and 39 other kids—all of them boys—learned how to read sports news on camera, how to write scripts for the programs, and how to interview athletes. Each broadcast team would get six weeks on the air.

Claire and a boy named Alex took turns being anchor and reporter. As the anchor, Claire read the week's sports news and scores and introduced reports. As a reporter, she interviewed athletes. Claire loved the work. She was nervous her first time on camera, but then she relaxed into the job.

Claire's parents and friends were proud of her. These days, though, Claire no longer says, "I'm going to be a sportscaster." Now she says, "I'm going to be a professional sportscaster." No one doubts her.

♦ Fill in the circle next to the correct answer.

7. When the woman at the TV station told Claire to get in line, Claire decided to _____ .

   ⓐ write a letter to the producer

   ⓑ give up trying for the job

   ⓒ ask her parents to write the producer

   ⓓ write the newspaper about the job

8. The producer decided to hire Claire because she _____ .

   ⓐ wanted the job   ⓑ wrote him a letter

   ⓒ was a good athlete   ⓓ knew a lot about sports

9. You can conclude from the story that some people think _____ .

   ⓐ kids should not be sportscasters

   ⓑ women cannot do a good job as sportscasters

   ⓒ men should not be sportscasters

   ⓓ women are better sportscasters than men

10. It is clear from the story that Claire _____ .

   ⓐ has a lot of friends   ⓑ is not easily discouraged

   ⓒ gets a lot of help   ⓓ is a good athlete

11. At first Claire was nervous, but she soon became more _____ .

   ⓐ awake   ⓑ relaxed

   ⓒ interesting   ⓓ forgetful

12. The station wanted kids to **broadcast** sports scores. To **broadcast** is to _____ .

   ⓐ announce on TV or radio   ⓑ research and compare

   ⓒ make corrections to   ⓓ copy on paper

Devin's Decision

"Your plate is too full, son," said Devin's father. Devin looked down at his dinner plate with a puzzled expression.

"What Dad means, is that you're involved in too many activities." said Devin's mother. "You have to make a choice."

Devin knew that his parents were right. He'd begun to feel squeezed, as if he were in a giant trash compactor. Devin was on a softball team and a swim team. He was a junior leader of Wilderness Scouts. He took piano lessons. Clearly, it was too much, but how could he decide what to give up?

The next morning, at swim practice, Devin asked himself, "Could I give this up?" He loved gliding through the cool water.

At softball practice after school, Devin thought to himself, "I like being with my friends and trying to hit home runs. Could I give this up?"

On Tuesday night, Devin helped lead a fire safety course in his Wilderness Scouts meeting. He tried to imagine giving up scouting.

On Thursday, at his piano lesson, Devin played his latest piece well. He was proud of himself.

At the end of the week, Devin announced his decision during dinner. "I've decided what I'll leave off my plate," he told his parents. "I'll drop softball this year. I can play it next year. I love swimming, but I don't have to be on a team. I can swim at the neighborhood pool anytime."

"As for piano lessons," Devin continued, "I'm definitely keeping them. I want to get better and better. To do that, I need lessons. I'm also staying in Wilderness Scouts. I'm learning things there that will probably come in handy later. Plus, I like being a leader."

"Well done, son," said Devin's dad.

"Thanks," said Devin. "So, now that my plate's not too full, would you please pass the potatoes?"

♦ Fill in the circle next to the correct answer.

13. Devin was feeling squeezed. He decided that he had to _____ .

   ⓐ join the swim team   ⓑ join the softball team

   ⓒ give up some activities   ⓓ give up piano lessons

14. Devin decided to stay in Wilderness Scouts so he could _____ .

   ⓐ learn about fire safety   ⓑ become president of the group

   ⓒ become a group leader   ⓓ learn skills to use all his life

15. Devin's parents wanted their son to _____ .

   ⓐ let them help him decide what to do

   ⓑ make his own decision about what to do

   ⓒ give up being on the swim team

   ⓓ give up being in Wilderness Scouts

16. Devin's decision clearly shows that he _____ .

   ⓐ wants to be a better swimmer   ⓑ is a good softball player

   ⓒ is a good leader   ⓓ wants to be a better piano player

17. Devin decided to **keep** some activities. The others he would have to

   _____ .

   ⓐ hold   ⓑ drop

   ⓒ learn   ⓓ add

18. At piano practice, Devin played his latest **piece**. The word **piece** in this sentence refers to _____ .

   ⓐ music   ⓑ calm

   ⓒ a little bit   ⓓ a puzzle

GO ON ▶

♦ Use the **outline** below to answer the following questions.

I. Stars
   A. constellations
   B. our night guides
   C. the sun is a star
   D. how stars live and die
   E. the Milky Way and other galaxies

II. Our Solar System
   A. planets
   B. moons
   C. the asteroid belt
   D. space exploration

III. The Universe
   A. measuring the universe
   B. space exploration

♦ Fill in the circle next to the correct answer.

19. In which section does the topic "Mars" belong?

   ⓐ the sun is a star   ⓑ planets

   ⓒ moons   ⓓ the Big Bang

20. What is a good title for a report based on this outline?

   ⓐ All About Space   ⓑ Halley's Comet

   ⓒ Venus   ⓓ Stars

GO ON ▶

♦ Use the **reference sources** below to answer the following questions.

♦ Fill in the circle next to the correct answer.

21. The sample entry of synonyms for "little" comes from _____ .

    ⓐ an atlas   ⓑ an encyclopedia

    ⓒ a dictionary   ⓓ a thesaurus

22. Which reference source would you choose if you wanted to see a map of Mexico?

    ⓐ an almanac   ⓑ an atlas

    ⓒ a dictionary   ⓓ a thesaurus

GO ON ▶

♦ Fill in the circle next to the correct answer.

23. Cowboy life was far from **glamorous**. The word **glamorous** means
_____ .

    ⓐ boring   ⓑ attractive

    ⓒ unappealing   ⓓ harsh

24. This passage is mainly about _____ .

    ⓐ how cattle stampede

    ⓑ moving cattle over long distances

    ⓒ how difficult the cowboy life can be

    ⓓ how young cowboys get work

25. You might guess that the youngest cowboys _____ .

    ⓐ get the worst jobs   ⓑ get the most food

    ⓒ take care of the youngest cows   ⓓ ride the best horses

GO ON ➡

♦ Imagine that your family's car could talk. What do you think it would say? Write a story about a day in the life of your car from your car's point of view.

_____

_____

_____

_____

_____

_____

_____

_____

_____

_____

_____

_____

_____

_____

_____

_____

_____

_____

_____

EVALUATION CHART
GRADE FIVE

UNIT 6: *Crossroads*

Student Name		Date	
Reading			
COMPREHENSION STRATEGIES		/ 12	%
Judgments and Decisions 7, 8, 13, 14			
Draw Conclusions 9, 10, 15, 16			
Cause and Effect 3, 4			
Sequence of Events 1, 2			
VOCABULARY STRATEGIES		/ 6	%
Context Clues 5, 6			
Antonyms and Synonyms 11, 12, 17, 18			
Study Skills		/ 4	%
Choose a Resource 19 - 22			
Listening Comprehension 23–25		/ 3	%
Constructing Meaning			
(Total of above three domains)			
Open-Ended Prompts/Written Response			
Writing: Story			
4 = Excellent			
3 = Good			
2 = Fair			
1 = Poor			
0 = Blank			
UNIT PERFORMANCE ASSESSMENT			
4 = Excellent			
3 = Good			
2 = Fair			
1 = Poor			

McGraw-Hill School Division
A Division of The McGraw-Hill Companies

McGraw-Hill School Division
Two Penn Plaza
New York, New York 10121
Printed in the United States of America
ISBN 0-02-185485-8
1 2 3 4 5 6 7 8 9 XXX 04 3 02 01 00 99

ISBN 0-02-185485-8
99701
9 780021 854851

5, U. 6

McGRAW-HILL READING

End-Year Test

Student Name: _____

Date: _____

Grade 5

A Thrilling Ride

When thrill-seekers first sit down in the roller coaster cars, their hearts begin to race. They take off slowly, but they see a giant hill looming in front of them. Click, click, click, and they're almost to the top. Suddenly, the car shoots down the hill, sending the riders through a hair-raising series of twists and turns. Before they know it, they're back to where they started. What a ride!

Roller coasters have existed for hundreds of years. Some coasters are made of wood, while others are made of steel. Some coasters are designed to be ridden while sitting, but others are made for standing. Roller coasters can take you backwards, forwards, or free-falling towards the earth.

However, the first roller coasters weren't so sophisticated. The first known record of a roller coaster dates back to the 1400s. People in Russia made large wooden slides that were covered with ice during winter. They called them Russian Mountains. Riders would climb an endless set of stairs to enjoy a quick ride down. Over the next 200 years, people built larger and larger slides. They became popular in other countries, too.

In the United States, however, people weren't interested in such rides. That changed when, in 1885, the owners of the Mauch Chuck Railway took their system for moving coal and changed it into a ride for passengers. People paid one dollar to ride the hour and a half, eighteen-mile coast downhill. After that, the demand for faster rides increased. People invented new designs for roller coasters.

Today coasters can go up to 100 miles per hour and drop over 200 feet. All this can be done without an engine. At the beginning of the ride, the car is pulled to the top of the first hill. But after that, the coaster finishes the ride using its own momentum. The cars are neither pushed along the track by a motor nor pulled by a hitch. All the energy needed to propel the coaster throughout the ride is achieved when the coaster goes down the first hill.

The roller coasters of today are very different from the original Russian Mountains. It seems people are always searching for coasters that are even bigger, faster, and scarier.

♦ Fill in the circle next to the correct answer.

1. What can you conclude about roller coasters of the future?

   ⓐ They'll get smaller and slower. ⓑ They'll get bigger and slower.

   ⓒ They'll get smaller and faster. ⓓ They'll get bigger and faster.

2. Which of the following explains why roller coasters don't need engines?

   ⓐ They are covered in ice. ⓑ They are pushed by a motor.

   ⓒ They use their own momentum. ⓓ They are just large wooden slides.

3. Which of the following is a fact from this story?

   ⓐ Roller coasters have existed for thousands of years.

   ⓑ The Russian Mountains were made of steel.

   ⓒ Roller coasters date back to the 1400s.

   ⓓ Motors always propel coasters throughout the ride.

4. What do a Russian Mountain and a modern coaster have in common?

   ⓐ People have found both exciting. ⓑ The rider stands on both of them.

   ⓒ They both are made of steel. ⓓ The engines of both are powerful.

5. Which ride was created first?

   ⓐ a 100 mile per hour roller coaster ⓑ a roller coaster that drops over 200 feet

   ⓒ an eighteen-mile roller coaster ⓓ a Russian Mountain

6. The author wrote this article to _____ .

   ⓐ warn the reader of the dangers of roller coasters

   ⓑ explain why roller coasters are the best of all rides

   ⓒ tell about the history of the roller coaster

   ⓓ tell about carnival rides of the 1400s

GO ON ➤

♦ Fill in the circle next to the correct answer.

7. It would be _____ to take an infant on a roller coaster.

    ⓐ thoughtful   ⓑ thoughtless

    ⓒ thoughtfulness   ⓓ thoughtfully

8. There is a lot of _____ on a roller coaster ride.

    ⓐ excitement   ⓑ exciting

    ⓒ excitable   ⓓ excitedly

9. I was awake all night thinking about my friend's **hair–raising** story. What does the word **hair–raising** mean?

    ⓐ boring   ⓑ scary

    ⓒ sad   ⓓ true

10. The boat's motor will **propel** it through the water. What does the word **propel** mean?

    ⓐ pull down   ⓑ cause to move

    ⓒ stay in place   ⓓ keep afloat

GO ON ▶

My Business Plan

Do you like guitars? I do, and I really want to learn how to play one. The problem is, I don't even have a guitar. My mom said if I save the money to purchase one, she would pay for music lessons. Now, I need a plan to earn the money.

Last summer, I tried to earn money to buy a new basketball goal for my driveway. I decided to wash cars to earn the money. My mom bought all the supplies for me: a red bucket, sponges, car wash liquid, and drying towels. I washed a lot of cars but still did not earn the $200 I needed for the goal. Instead, I spent the money I did manage to earn on new soccer equipment.

Because the guitar I've picked out costs $300, I know the car wash business won't earn enough. So this time I'm going to try lawn care. Two summers ago, my Dad taught me how to mow our lawn. He paid me fifteen dollars each time I mowed. When the idea of lawn care first came to me, I did some research on our street by talking to the neighbors. I learned that some of them don't have enough time to mow their yards and that some of them dislike the chore. Almost all of them agreed that it would be a wonderful service to have their lawns mowed for them.

Six of my neighbors told me right then that they will hire me to mow their grass. They will pay me fifteen dollars each time I mow. I anticipate each yard will need to be mowed every seven days. Multiplication shows I'll probably earn $90 a week; that's $270 in three weeks. Even though Dad says I have to pay for the gasoline for the mower, I should be able to purchase my guitar in less than two months!

I'm looking forward to the summer. It's going to feel great to select my guitar at the store and purchase it with my own hard-earned money. I'm confident that my business plan will work.

♦ Fill in the circle next to the correct answer.

11. When the narrator wanted a basketball goal he decided to _____ .

ⓐ baby-sit   ⓑ wash cars

ⓒ mow lawns   ⓓ walk dogs

12. What can you tell about the narrator by reading this story?

ⓐ He is lazy.   ⓑ He can't save money.

ⓒ He is hardworking.   ⓓ He's a good musician.

13. The narrator wants to buy a guitar. How will he solve this problem?

ⓐ His mom will pay for it.   ⓑ He'll wash cars to earn money.

ⓒ He'll mow his lawn for his Dad.   ⓓ He'll mow his neighbor's lawns to earn money.

14. Which piece of information is **not** important to the story?

ⓐ The narrator wants a guitar.   ⓑ The bucket was red.

ⓒ The narrator pays for the gas.   ⓓ The narrator will mow lawns.

15. Why did the narrator decide to mow lawns instead of wash cars this summer?

ⓐ Washing cars was too boring.

ⓑ The supplies for washing cars were too expensive.

ⓒ His mom won't buy him a new bucket.

ⓓ He can't earn enough money by washing cars.

16. The narrator wants to mow lawns this summer in order to _____ .

ⓐ buy a guitar   ⓑ buy a basketball goal

ⓒ save for college   ⓓ pay for music lessons

♦ Fill in the circle next to the correct answer.

17. All of the neighbors _____ the loud, barking dog.

    ⓐ disagree   ⓑ dislike

    ⓒ unhappy   ⓓ deplete

18. He _____ the numbers to see how much he will earn.

    ⓐ multiplication   ⓑ multiplied

    ⓒ multiple   ⓓ multiplier

19. You should **anticipate** a long wait in line at the new movie. What does the word **anticipate** mean?

    ⓐ ignore   ⓑ appreciate

    ⓒ be prepared for   ⓓ be happy about

20. I feel **confident** that I'll make a good grade on the test. What does the word **confident** mean?

    ⓐ afraid   ⓑ bad

    ⓒ happy   ⓓ sure of success

GO ON ▶

Rolling Racers

It was Manisha's first day to sit up after her ankle surgery. With the help of Mr. Baca, her favorite nurse, she was sitting in a wheelchair with both legs extended in front of her like a pair of cannons. Mr. Baca pushed her chair around the third floor of the hospital. Manisha was glad to get a change of scenery from her room, where she'd memorized all her speedy recovery cards.

Mr. Baca pushed Manisha into the sunroom. The light was dazzling. The ferns cast shadows on the couch and tile floor. He handed her two magazines and said, "Enjoy the sunshine. I'll be back for you in a little while."

"Oh, Mr. Baca, this is the most beautiful room in the hospital!"

Manisha flipped through the magazines. Then, she heard children's voices in the hall. She cautiously rolled one wheel backwards and the chair began to turn. It took all the strength she could muster to roll the chair across the room. Manisha could not believe how feeble her arms felt.

Two boys were in wheelchairs in the hall. The taller boy had an IV hooked up to the back of his chair that rolled with him. They lined up side by side, and the smaller boy said, "On your mark. Get set. Go!" And the two of them raced down the hall!

Manisha laughed, amazed at how fast they made those chairs roll. The tall boy introduced himself as Garrett, and the winner's name was Alex. The boys showed Manisha how to reach farther back and give the wheel a push; she discovered that she could move farther on one efficient push. She spent the next two days practicing whenever she could.

By the third day, Manisha decided she had practiced long enough. She was ready to challenge Alex and Garrett to a race. First, they raced from the nurse's station, down the corridor to Garrett's room. Garrett won. Then, they raced to the sunroom. Manisha gave it all she could. She thought about her first day in the sunroom and she pushed harder and harder. With her legs thrust out in front of her, Manisha's feet crossed the doorway first. The three children slapped hands, each happy for the progress they'd made.

Name _____ Date _____

♦ Fill in the circle next to the correct answer.

21. You can tell that Manisha _____ during her stay at the hospital.

ⓐ had fun   ⓑ made no friends

ⓒ didn't like the nurses   ⓓ became sicker

22. The following is important to the story: Manisha _____ .

ⓐ liked Mr. Baca   ⓑ looked at two magazines

ⓒ practiced for two days   ⓓ sat in the sunroom

23. Before Alex said, "On your mark. Get set. Go!" _____ .

ⓐ the boys showed Manisha how to push efficiently

ⓑ the boys lined up side by side

ⓒ Manisha challenged the boys to a race

ⓓ Manisha practiced for two days

24. It is a fact that _____ .

ⓐ Mr. Baca is a doctor   ⓑ Manisha won the last race

ⓒ Garret had ankle surgery   ⓓ Manisha didn't get any cards

25. Manisha made the judgment that the sunroom was the most beautiful room because _____ .

ⓐ it had speedy recovery cards

ⓑ it was filled with dazzling light and ferns

ⓒ Mr. Baca took her there

ⓓ she heard children's voices there

26. Manisha decided to race Alex and Garrett because _____ .

ⓐ she knew she would win   ⓑ she had practiced enough

ⓒ she was bored   ⓓ she wanted to go to the sunroom

♦ Fill in the circle next to the correct answer.

27. Manisha spent a _____ night reading a book.

    ⓐ sleepiness   ⓑ sleeper

    ⓒ sleepwalk   ⓓ sleepless

28. The athlete completed all three events in the _____ .

    ⓐ pentathlon   ⓑ heptagon

    ⓒ decathlon   ⓓ triathlon

29. The children rolled down the **corridor**. A synonym for the word **corridor** is _____ .

    ⓐ room   ⓑ hallway

    ⓒ ramp   ⓓ hospital

30. Manisha's arms were **feeble** at first. An antonym for the word **feeble** is _____ .

    ⓐ foolish   ⓑ weak

    ⓒ feel   ⓓ strong

GO ON ▶

A Baseball Legend

Jackie Robinson is a man who changed professional sports forever. In 1947, he became the first African American to play professional baseball for a major league team. Although he was a great athlete, he dealt with a lot of pressure from people who did not want an African American to play on the same team as Caucasians.

Jackie Robinson was born on January 31, 1919, in Cairo, Georgia. He went to UCLA. There he lettered in four different sports: football, basketball, baseball, and track. That accomplishment has yet to be repeated by any other athlete at the school. After college, he joined the Negro Baseball League. At that time, both the professional basketball and football teams still wouldn't allow African-American players to join their teams.

Jackie played in the Negro League until he joined the Brooklyn Dodgers on August 28, 1945. In 1946 he hit his first home run. When he returned to the dugout, not a single player congratulated him. That's the kind of racial prejudice Jackie fought everyday.

In his first season, Jackie led the league in stolen bases. As a second baseman he led the league in fielding. His lifetime on-base percentage is .410. That percentage is number 25 on the all-time list. In 1955, he led the Dodgers to win the World Series.

Although he achieved all these accomplishments, Jackie always dealt with hatred. He got letters from people who said they would kill him if he continued to play. Those people didn't want him to play on the same field with white players. He was a courageous man to continue playing baseball.

Jackie Robinson was the first African-American player to play professionally outside the Negro League, but that's not the only thing that made him special. His speed and power made the game exciting to watch. He was the first African American to win the Rookie of the Year award, win a batting title, play in the World Series, and be inducted into the Hall of Fame. He did all this while fighting racial prejudice. He is truly a baseball legend.

♦ Fill in the circle next to the correct answer.

31. You can tell that the author thinks that _____ .

   ⓐ what Jackie Robinson did was easy

   ⓑ what Jackie Robinson did was not important

   ⓒ Jackie Robinson should be admired

   ⓓ Jackie Robinson is just like any other baseball player

32. Compared to the other players, Jackie Robinson was _____ .

   ⓐ taller   ⓑ not treated the same

   ⓒ not as good of a baseball player   ⓓ younger

33. The problem Jackie faced was _____ .

   ⓐ racial prejudice   ⓑ he was not a good baseman

   ⓒ he was not a good batter   ⓓ he didn't know how to play baseball

34. You can conclude that Jackie Robinson's name is _____ .

   ⓐ in record books   ⓑ often misspelled

   ⓒ unknown   ⓓ forgotten

35. After reading this story you can correctly say that _____ .

   ⓐ African Americans and Caucasians were treated equally in the 1940s

   ⓑ baseball is boring

   ⓒ people didn't like baseball

   ⓓ many fans were upset that an African American was playing with whites

36. You can conclude that Jackie Robinson _____ .

   ⓐ was an only child   ⓑ liked football more than baseball

   ⓒ was a good athlete   ⓓ didn't enjoy baseball

♦ If you could dig a hole to the center of the Earth you would discover that the Earth is made of four layers. The diagram below shows the Earth's four layers. Use the **diagram** to answer the questions on the next page.

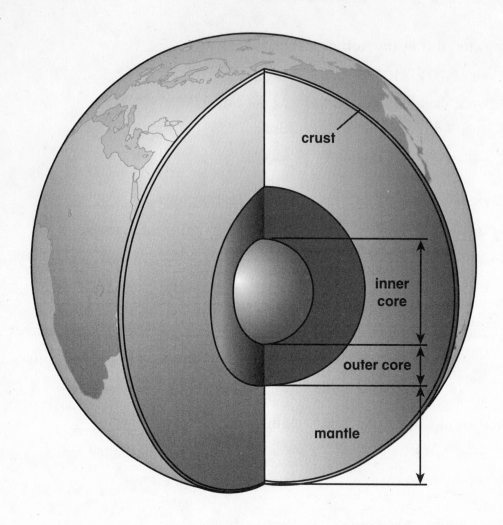

crust

inner core

outer core

mantle

Name _____ Date _____

♦ Fill in the circle next to the correct answer.

37. Which layer is the thinnest?
    ⓐ crust   ⓑ mantle
    ⓒ outer core   ⓓ inner core

38. Which layer is in the center of the earth?
    ⓐ crust   ⓑ mantle
    ⓒ outer core   ⓓ inner core

39. Which layer is next to the crust?
    ⓐ inner core   ⓑ outer core
    ⓒ middle core   ⓓ mantle

GO ON ▶

♦ A **news article** is pictured below. Use the information to answer the questions on the next page.

THE CITY NEWSPAPER

Sunny City   Monday, Aug. 16

No More Summers for Children
by Sue Smiley

Sunny City, Monday, Aug. 16, 1999

The Sunny City School Board voted last night to stop having summer vacations for the Sunny City School District. The decision was made to try to make the students learn more.

The School Board members were concerned that during the summer months the students were having too much fun and forgetting what they had learned during the school year. Mr. Principal, a school board member said, "We want Sunny City students to be the best they can be. If they are in school all year, they will learn more."

People had different reactions to the School Board's decision. One parent responded, "I think it is great. My child should be in school longer."

Susie Subject, fifth grader said, "I think it's terrible. We deserve a break after being in school for nine months."

Beginning with this school year, the Sunny City students will be going to school year round.

♦ Fill in the circle next to the correct answer.

40. What is the headline of this news article?

ⓐ The City News   ⓑ Sunny City

ⓒ No More Summers for Children   ⓓ Sue Smiley

41. What is the main idea of the article?

ⓐ Children love school in Sunny City.

ⓑ The School Board voted to close school in Sunny City.

ⓒ The children wanted to build a playground at their school.

ⓓ The School Board voted to have year round school in Sunny City.

42. Who voted to make school year round?

ⓐ Mr. Principal   ⓑ Sue Smiley

ⓒ Susie Subject   ⓓ Sunny

GO ON ▶

♦ Below are notes on **how to conduct an interview**. Use the information to answer the questions on the next page.

Speaking and Listening Guidelines:

An Interview
- State the purpose of the interview clearly.
- Be polite. Ask questions simply and directly.
- Listen closely to the answers and take notes about them.
- Ask questions to get more information about an answer.

Name _____ Date _____

♦ Fill in the circle next to the correct answer.

43. How should you ask questions in an interview?

   ⓐ quickly   ⓑ very slowly

   ⓒ directly   ⓓ impatiently

44. What should you do if you want more information about an answer given?

   ⓐ Ask follow up questions.

   ⓑ Pretend you know the answer.

   ⓒ Ask the person to repeat what's been said.

   ⓓ Don't ask any more questions.

45. What should you do during an interview?

   ⓐ Make up questions to ask.

   ⓑ Draw a picture of the person you're interviewing.

   ⓒ Listen carefully and take notes.

   ⓓ Plan your day.

GO ON ▶

Name _____ Date _____

♦ Fill in the circle next to the correct answer.

46. My mom says not to worry so much. She says everything will go **swimmingly**. What does the word **swimmingly** mean?

ⓐ slowly   ⓑ badly
ⓒ fine   ⓓ wet

47. What is the one good thing about Carver Middle School?

ⓐ It's all the way across town.   ⓑ It has a swim team.
ⓒ It's huge.   ⓓ Her friends won't be there.

48. What did the narrator worry about all summer?

ⓐ beginning middle school   ⓑ moving to a new city
ⓒ staying in elementary school   ⓓ walking to school

49. How did the narrator feel about Carver Middle School at the end of the story?

ⓐ She was uninterested in it.   ⓑ She was more nervous than before.

ⓒ She didn't like it.   ⓓ She wasn't nervous. She liked it.

50. What happened when the narrator boarded the school bus?

ⓐ She missed it.   ⓑ She cried.
ⓒ She saw her friend April.   ⓓ She sat next to a new girl.

GO ON ▶

- ◆ Write an essay about three good things about your school. Include facts and details.
- ◆ Write an essay comparing yourself to the girl in the story. How would you feel about starting middle school? Why? How did she feel?
- ◆ Make up a story about someone facing his or her fears and doing something for the first time. What is the person nervous about? How does he or she overcome the fear?

_____

_____

_____

_____

_____

_____

_____

_____

_____

_____

_____

_____

_____

_____

_____

_____

_____

EVALUATION CHART

GRADE FIVE

END-YEAR TEST SCORING

Student Name _____	Date _____		
Reading			
COMPREHENSION STRATEGIES 1–6, 11–16, 21–26, 31–36		/24	%
VOCABULARY STRATEGIES 7–10, 17–20, 27–30		/12	%
Study Skills/Information Resources 37–45		/9	%
Listening Comprehension 46–50		/5	%
Open-Ended Prompts/Written Response			
Writing			
4 = Excellent			
3 = Good			
2 = Fair			
1 = Poor			
0 = Blank			

McGraw-Hill School Division
A Division of The McGraw-Hill Companies

McGraw-Hill School Division
Two Penn Plaza
New York, New York 10121
Printed in the United States of America
ISBN 0-02-185515-3
1 2 3 4 5 6 7 8 9 024 04 3 02 01 00 99

ISBN 0-02-185515-3

99701

9 780021 855155

5